Jack Nicholson

Books by Donald Shepherd

Nonfiction

Alone with Me
with Eartha Kitt

Bing Crosby: The Hollow Man
with Robert F. Slatzer

Bogie and Me
with Verita Thompson

Duke: The Life and Times of John Wayne
with Slatzer and Dave Grayson

Jack Nicholson: An Unauthorized Biography

Fiction

Dark Eden
The Key
Darkness Falling
A Cool and Restless Flame
The Devil's Vineyard

Donald Shepherd

Jack Nicholson

An
Unauthorized
Biography

St. Martin's Press
New York

Design by Dawn Niles

Library of Congress Cataloging-in-Publication Data

Shepherd, Donald.
    Jack Nicholson : an unauthorized biography / Donald Shepherd.
        p.   cm.
    "A Thomas Dunne book."
    ISBN 0-312-05449-1
    1. Nicholson, Jack.   2. Motion picture actors and actresses—
United States—Biography.   I. Title.
PN2287.N5S54   1991
791.43'028'092—dc20
    [B]   90-48996
                                                                    CIP

First Edition: June 1991
10 9 8 7 6 5 4 3 2 1

for Michael Brian Shepherd, Sr.,
and for Tina and Mikey

CONTENTS

May I sit on
your chair,
share your food
when you eat,
and lie on your
bed when I'm
tired?

From *The Frog Prince*

Jack Nicholson

Jack Nicholson was thirty-seven years old in the summer of 1974. He was stocky and had to watch his weight, and his hairline was receding above a pleasant but ordinary Irish face. On screen and off, he spoke with a soft, flat-toned rhythmic drawl, and seemed an unlikely candidate for leading-man roles, much less stardom. Yet there he was, a star on the threshold of super-stardom, looking bemused and, as one *Time* mag-azine writer observed, "Like an all-night coach passenger who is just beginning to realize he has slept through his stop."

He was featured on the cover of *Time* that Au-gust. The cover story called him "the star with the killer smile" and "a sort of cutup prince re-gent," and intimated that he was a klieg-light rebel who had somehow drifted into the filmic mainstream he had been trying to avoid. It was a

1

FAMILY SECRET 1974

widely accepted image of him then, but not a true one. There was nothing Jack had wanted more than to be a film star in the traditional sense—one within the studio system and with all its privileges, its limousines and bright lights and best tables. He was drawn to such stuff; he loved it, found it irresistible. It was the entertainment media that had dubbed him a rebel, despite evidence to the contrary. In fact, he was a practitioner of the Hollywood game: Like the good pool player he once was, he flashed his smile, calculated the angles, and gave Hollywood his best shot. But after fifteen frustrating years he decided to give up acting and to focus on directing. It was only then, and by accident, that he wafted to stardom on a marijuana haze.

Time noted that while he had gained popularity as a film actor for his role in *Easy Rider* five years earlier, it wasn't until 1974 that he began experiencing the first flush of excitement at being a household name. He was now among the most sought-after actors in Hollywood. Directors like Elia Kazan, Stanley Kubrick, Bernardo Bertolucci, and Michelangelo Antonioni were, or would be, seeking an audience with him. *Time* reported that not since the "burnished 30s" had Hollywood become so big-name conscious as it was with this late-bloomer from Neptune City, New Jersey.

He had been nominated for an Academy Award as Best Supporting Actor for his work in *Easy Rider*, and had proved worthy of that attention by thereafter giving solid and interesting performances in films such as *Five Easy Pieces, Carnal Knowledge, The King of Marvin Gardens, The Last Detail*, and *Chinatown*. He had received Best Actor nominations for his work in three of them. He was at work on his twenty-ninth film, *The Fortune*, when staff members of *Time* turned their attention to him in that late summer of 1974; it was while researching his background for their cover story that they discovered a family secret and confronted him with it by phone. They learned that the family had kept the secret from Jack, too.

He was on the movie set when he received the phone call, presumably from a member of the magazine's research staff. He usually avoided the distractions of interviewers and other outsiders while working, but the prospect of having his photograph on the cover of *Time* and of being the cover-story subject was an extraordinary and intoxicating experience, and so he took the call and was faced with the reality that Ethel May Nicholson, whom he had always thought to be his mother, was his grandmother; that his namesake, John Joseph Nicholson, was not his father, but his grandfather; that his youngest "sister," Lorraine, was his aunt; and that June Nicholson, the woman he had believed for thirty-seven years to be his elder sister, was his natural mother.

Jack was stunned. "Since I was at work," he said, "I went to Mike Nichols, the director, and said, 'Now, Mike, you know I'm a big-time Method actor: I just found out something—something just came through, so keep an eye on me. Don't let me get away with anything.' "[2] He later called Lorraine in New Jersey, who verified the discovery. She was the only family member who could; June, John, and Ethel May were dead by then. They had taken their secret, including the identity of Jack's father, to their graves; apparently, not even Lorraine knew who Jack's father was.

Jack asked the magazine's editors not to print their findings. His request was honored. It would be another decade (1984) before the secret would surface once more and he would allow it to be made public. "Yes," he said, when confronted again, "these are the circumstances of my life."[3]

Although he has never gone into detail about those circumstances, there is evidence that June Nicholson was not only unwed but also very young when she gave birth—perhaps in her early teens.[4] In any event, the introduction of an infant into the Nicholson household under such strained conditions undoubtedly had an unsettling effect. Certainly Ethel May regarded her own circumstances with ambivalence; she was middle-aged, her marriage had foundered, and times were hard. Even so, she raised Jack as her own, while June went on with her life as though Jack was not her child.

Despite his shock at the revelation, and while he had naturally turned to Lorraine to verify the facts, there is no indication that he doubted what the researchers had discovered about his birth. Indeed, the revelation reinforced and put into perspective many deeply felt but vague impressions that had apparently always troubled him about his childhood and his familial relationships. It gave new insight and validity to an eerie experience he had had in the early 1960s, as well. He went to an analyst then and was among the first to experiment with the hallucinogen LSD under clinical

3

supervision. One effect of the drug was that he "relived" his birth and disturbing impressions of infancy, an experience that he had tried to reconcile with what he then perceived as the reality of his past, but which must have left puzzling gaps until the family secret was made known to him. During an interview that was conducted two years before he learned the truth of his birth (and ten years after his drug-induced experience), he gave a graphic account of the sensations he had experienced, and then added, "I became conscious of very early emotions about not being wanted—feeling that I was a problem to my family as an infant."[5] He interpreted the feelings at the time as owing to the separation of his "parents" (actually his grandparents) shortly before his birth; however, in an interview conducted a year after he learned that June was his natural mother, he said of the drug-induced experience, "I got back to the terrible realization I had as an infant: that my mother didn't want me."[6]

4

> "Let's just say I
> was presented
> the Pimple
> Award and
> every other
> kind of gross-
> out award in
> my youth."
>
> *Jack Nicholson*[1]

I t was on April 22, 1937, that June Nicholson, unwed daughter of Ethel May and John Joseph Nicholson, gave birth to a baby boy in New York City, where she had gone to have the child.[2] It was decided that her mother would raise the offspring as her own, so June named him John Joseph Nicholson, Jr. Shortly thereafter, she returned to the Nicholson home in Neptune, New Jersey, where she placed the infant in Ethel May's care and where he spent his childhood raised in the belief that Ethel May and John were his parents and that June and her younger sister, Lorraine, were his sisters.

The Nicholson household changed considerably after Jackie, as he was called, was brought home. Ethel May and John had found it increasingly difficult to resolve their differences, and they had separated permanently just before Jackie's

2

NEPTUNE CITY AND SPRING LAKE

birth. John Nicholson was a kind and charming Irishman, a self-employed window dresser and sign painter by trade, who was often chosen one of the best-dressed men in the Asbury Park, New Jersey, Easter Parade in his younger days. By the time Jackie arrived, John was afflicted with alcoholism and was out of control, slowly drinking himself to death. Even though he remained in Neptune after his separation from Ethel May, he was seldom seen by his family. He did visit his daughters on occasion, though, and sometimes took Jackie along on his rounds of the city's beer gardens. "He was an incredible drinker," Jack said. "I would drink eighteen sarsaparillas while he'd have thirty-five shots of three-star Hennessy. But I never heard him raise his voice; I never saw anybody angry with him, not even my mother [Ethel May]. He was just a quiet, melancholy, tragic figure—a very soft man."[3]

John was still around when Jack was in high school. A high school pal, George Anderson, remembered one occasion when Jack spoke of him. "I knew his father was an alcoholic," Anderson said, "but the only time Jack mentioned him was one day when he said, 'I saw my father yesterday. The poor guy; I feel sorry for him because he can't help it.' "[4]

With John so afflicted and absent from the household, the burden of supporting their two teenage daughters and the infant addition to the family fell to Ethel May. It was a task made more difficult by hard times in those late Depression years, but Ethel May was determined, resourceful, and independent; she had been born to a wealthy Pennsylvania Dutch Protestant family that disinherited her for marrying young and to an Irish Catholic. She rose to the new challenge. She heard of a company in nearby Newark that sold permanent-wave machines and offered a course in cosmetology to anyone who bought one. Ethel May bought a machine, took the course to become a beautician, and opened a neighborhood beauty parlor in a bedroom of their rented house. Considering the times, she did very well as the family breadwinner, and it wasn't long before she moved her family to a larger, two-story house at 1410 Sixth Avenue, in a better quarter of town—called Neptune City —than John Nicholson had been able to afford. "I was never an underprivileged kid," Jack said. "My grandmother/mother was a very strong, independent lady who made her own living. She was also smart in terms of where we lived. In Neptune, there was a slightly rougher, lower-middle-class region and a more upper-middle-class one. Ethel May Nicholson was smart enough to move her children to the better area—and cover it. So I never felt poor; in fact, quite the opposite."[5]

Jack was surrounded by women from infancy. There were Ethel May, June, and Lorraine, all of whom watched over him, and there was the daily gathering of Ethel May's female clients. Home to Jack was perm machines and hair dryers, the acrid smell of bleach and perm solutions, and the intimate, often earthy talk of women. As a result, he grew up with a better appreciation of the female condition and of life from the female perspective than most males are ever privy to, and he would later move among women with an uncommon ease and a genuine interest that often caused even his most casual of female friends to seek him as a confidant.

It wasn't until Lorraine married that Jack had a male role model to lend a semblance of balance to his formative years in Neptune. Lorraine and George Smith, or "Shorty," as Jack nicknamed him, had been childhood sweethearts from the time Lorraine was seven and Shorty eleven. They married young, and Shorty moved into the Sixth Avenue house when Jack was two or three. Shorty had been an outstanding athlete—a football star—in his school days, and he was known and loved in Neptune. He was a good man, a railroad brakeman by trade. Shorty would never have presumed to serve as a father figure for Jack, but Jack considered him so. "There's nobody much that's impressed me as much as Shorty," Jack has said. "Simple guy, but many is the poem I've written in my mind to the higher feelings he promoted in me."[6] Jack would one day employ Shorty in films; they remained very close until Shorty's death in 1985.

June was the restless flame of the Nicholson clan. Mature and wise beyond her years, she was also pretty, independent, and ambitious. She apparently had studied dance and had a talent for it, and she left home to pursue a show-business career when Jack was four. She became an Earl Carroll dancer in New York City and Miami, and later is said to have worked as a straight woman for comedian Pinky Lee, a former vaudevillian who was headlining for Earl Carroll at the time. As the show-business "star" of the family, June was an inspiration to young Jack. "She was a symbol of excitement, thrilling and beautiful to me," he once said. The fact that June had a nodding acquaintance with entertainment notables and even with underworld figures such as Lucky Luciano fascinated Jack, too. He has never gotten over his awe of famous, notorious, and glamorous people. Although Jack had no show-business aspirations himself, the feeling that he might be destined for something beyond the workaday life of Neptune City came to him early in childhood. Such stirrings were vague, though, and so apparently beyond the reality of his circumstances that he paid them little attention.

Jack barely had reached the toddler stage when he began exhibiting a stubborn, independent streak like his mother's. Perhaps owing to the extraordinary elements of his birth, and therefore to his subconscious sense of being an intruder in his own family—and, by extension, in society, as well—his independent streak was complicated by an inordinate need for acceptance and belonging. His family must have found his seemingly contradictory signals bewildering.

Jack's strong need for attention was manifested early, by spectacular tantrums: the lying on the floor, red-faced, kicking and screaming kind. Then as an adolescent, he was not reluctant to parade his anger before Ethel May's startled clients by rumbling through the house, stomping up the stairs, slamming doors like cannon shots, and bellowing loudly at the injustice of not always getting his own way—even though Ethel May seldom refused him anything. As he matured, he found charm a more effective means of manipulation, and he cultivated a more subtle and socially acceptable repertoire of personality traits that assured him attention and that have become characteristic of him: an infectious, disarming smile; an ingratiating manner; a charming, almost hypnotically intimate manner of speech; a knack for getting along with people and for making them laugh; and a habit of nicknaming people. By giving family and friends private, pet names, he established an apparent intimate bond, thereby making them more accessible. He had special names for members of his family; he called Ethel May "Mud," Lorraine "Rain," and George "Shorty."

Jack entered Roosevelt Grammar School in September 1943, and made his stage debut there a few years later—at age ten—singing or lip-synching "Managua, Nicaragua," a popular song of the day. He was a bright but undisciplined and unmotivated student. Even after he skipped a grade at Roosevelt, his studies held no challenge for him. "I enjoyed school," he said, "but I wasn't into learning. I met the requirements in order to enjoy what I liked about school—being around a lot of people and having a good time."[7] He was not particularly respectful of authority, at home or elsewhere. He has always found officious people offensive, calling them the "head ushers" of the world. His childhood rebelliousness was usually nonconfrontational, though; he devised ways of skirting rather than challenging authority. Even so, his attitude caused what he called "deportment problems" in school, minor ones, mostly, but frequent and sometimes serious enough to get him temporarily expelled on more than one occasion.

By the time he reached the sixth or seventh grade, Jack was pushing for independence at home, too. Ethel May was permissive by nature and Jack was stubborn and self-indulgent, so she gave him relatively free rein, telling him that he was on his own and requiring only that he tell her whether he got into trouble. "I was the only kid in school who never *had* to go home," he said, "as long as I called to let them know I was all right."[8] Ethel May kept a box of pennies in her beauty salon that Jack could draw from when he pleased; he did so to attend movies, which he loved, often treating his friends. He also bought a lot of comic books, and later became an avid reader of novels.

When he was about eight, vistas outside Neptune opened to him. June had left the entertainment business during World War II to join the millions of women who entered the work force to help the war effort. She worked in the flight-control tower at Detroit, Michigan's Willow Run Airport, the military's central air-dispatching point. It was presumably at Willow Run that she met and fell in love with a young test pilot, the son of a wealthy East Coast surgeon. They married and eventually settled in Stony Brook, Long Island, where they raised a family, led a glamorous country-club life, and where Jack spent his summers playing with his half brothers and half sisters, thinking they were his nieces and nephews.[9]

June's husband was among the small group of pilots who tested the first air force jet fighter, and Jack was taken to see it. It was painted a vivid Day-Glo color so that it would be seen easily if it went down during its maiden flight over the polar ice cap. This was heady stuff for a young boy, an experience that led him to join the air force reserve when it later became necessary for him to fulfill his military obligation during those days when military conscription was in force.

Jack eagerly anticipated his summers at Stony Brook, but they ended during his high school years when June's marriage failed. She and the children moved back in with Ethel May and Jack and Shorty and Lorraine for a while, and she commuted to Manhattan, where she taught dancing at Arthur Murray's and presumably sought to revive her show-business career. Many of her contacts had gone west to Hollywood, however, including her old partner Pinky Lee, who had headlined at the Hollywood Earl Carroll Theatre, and so she loaded her children and belongings into her car and drove west. It was a courageous move in those days for a single woman with small children, but that's the way June was; she was too ambitious and adventurous to remain in Neptune.

In his early teens, Jack did the things all teenage boys did in those days, but given his relative independence and iconoclastic nature, he undoubtedly did them with extraordinary fervor and style. He hung around the pool hall a lot. And he grew chubby, if not fat. He claims to have been a candidate for the "Pimple Award and every other kind of gross-out award"; he seems to have turned even this awkward phase to advantage, taking pride in it. If he had to pass through such a phase, he intended to do so with gross style, thereby entertaining—and keeping—his friends, who were inordinately important to him. He learned how to maneuver himself into any group—even a peripheral position would do; it was belonging that counted. One high school pal talked of Jack's "terrific" smile and noted that unlike most of his classmates, who tended to run with their own peers, Jack had "plenty" of friendships that spanned all ages. He wasn't one of the school's campus heroes, but he was among the most prominent of cutups and partygoers, and he made it a point to be on friendly terms with the campus heroes in order to gain access to their circles.

Ethel May had moved the family to an apartment at 505 Mercer Avenue in Spring Lake by the time Jack reached high school. Spring Lake is a resort community a few miles south of Neptune, and it was there that Jack lived while attending Manasquan High School. He speaks fondly and ardently of his life and times at Spring Lake, and he so internalized the social affectations of the day as to become a personification of them. "This was the age of the put-on," he says. "Cool was everything. You never let on what bothered you."[10] He wore dark sunglasses, or "shades," as they were called, navy blue pegged pants, dark turtleneck sweaters, and a black porkpie hat, which had a mystique about it because it had been left at the scene of an automobile accident. He held a few part-time jobs while in high school, including one as a caddy for the local country club, but mostly he hung around with friends. They went to New York City on weekends to attend ball games or to get drunk. During the summer, he went to the beach and he drank every night—not much, but enough to relieve the peer pressure. He was a lifeguard one summer at Bradley Beach; his job was to man a dinghy just outside the breakers and keep swimmers near shore, or to haul them back in if they strayed. He used to row the boat standing up, wearing mirrored sunglasses and a black wool coat—despite the heat—a cool Catcher in the Rye. He is said to have performed a heroic deed that summer. There was a bad storm, with riptides so powerful that other lifeguards couldn't get their boats beyond them to save swimmers swept offshore. Jack managed to get his boat out and pick them up. A photo of the daring rescue is said to have been printed in the local paper. Jack said he got an attack of seasickness from his feat, and that what the photo didn't show was him vomiting afterward in front of the crowd that had gathered to watch the rescue.

Like most young men, Jack was a sports enthusiast and counted athletes such as Joe DiMaggio among his heroes. He played on the freshman football team, but his favorite team sport was, and is, basketball. He played freshman basketball, too, but he didn't make the varsity team the following year. Instead, he became its manager, a job that entailed tending equipment and whatever other odd jobs the coaches assigned him. His unbridled temper and fanatical team loyalty cost him any chance he may have had to participate in high school sports after his freshman year. Angered by what he perceived as an indignity to his team during a game away from home, he sneaked back into the opposing team's gymnasium after the game and wrecked the electronic scoreboard. He wasn't caught in the act, but his compulsion for telling the truth—if not bragging about the incident—led him to admit to the vandalism later. He had to find part-time jobs to pay for the damage he had caused, and he

11

was also banned from participating in sports for the remainder of his high school years. This infuriated him; without sports to occupy his time, he thought of other things to do that school administrators felt he ought not to, such as smoking on campus and being generally uncooperative.

His deportment was such that he was required to stay after school almost every day of his sophomore year, where he had to write essays as punishment. When he realized that his essays weren't being read word for word, he padded them with unkind editorial comments about his teachers and the school. He eventually tired of this and used the time honing his fiction-writing skills by creating adventures about a genie and his boy. "It's one of the few things I wish I could actually recover," Jack has said. "A genie and his boy—God knows what was influencing me at the time."[11]

He settled down a bit during his junior and senior years. He joined the Table-Tennis Club (and is still a formidable player), and was elected vice-president of his senior class. He acted in the junior and senior plays, and was voted both Best Actor and Class Clown by his peers.

Jack graduated from Manasquan in June of 1954 at age seventeen. He considered going to college, for he is said to have scored in the top 2 percentile on his College Boards and to have been offered financial assistance by the University of Delaware. The thought of becoming either a chemical engineer or a journalist appealed to him, but working for it did not. The idea of immediately buckling down to four years of hard study and of having to work his way through school wasn't what made an adventurous, rather indolent, and free-spirited young man's heart quicken, so he decided to put off considering college for at least a year, or until he satisfied the wanderlust that breaking free of public school stirred in him. Lorraine counseled him to widen his horizons. "If you stay around Neptune, where life is kind of easy and everyone knows you, you'll always be Jackie Nicholson," she told him, "but if you go somewhere else, you'll be what you accomplish."[12]

The only place outside Neptune where the newly graduated seventeen-year-old had close family ties was California, which is undoubtedly where Lorraine and Ethel May had been tactfully trying to steer him. This created an unanticipated problem, though, which must have caused the Nicholson women some anxious moments:

A young man striking out on his own would have to have proof of his identity and birth for legal purposes. Even if his birth was registered, the family obviously couldn't have put *that* certificate in Jack's hands. Therefore, Ethel May signed and filed a certificate of delayed report of birth a few weeks before his graduation, attesting that she and John Nicholson were his parents. With this document, Jack set out for California to visit June. Beyond that, he had no other plans.

"It was as
though some-
one would
come in with
this Jack Ni-
cholson man-
nequin and set
it down in the
booth with us
at Schwab's,
and it would
just sit there,
smiling."

John Gilmore[1]

June had apparently given up hope of making her mark in show business by the time Jack went to visit her in the summer of 1954. She had taken what was for her a mundane job. She would eventually make her career as an assistant buyer for the J. C. Penney department-store chain, but at this time she was working as an apprentice secretary in the office of an aircraft plant.

Jack stayed for about six months with her and her children in Inglewood, a Los Angeles suburb about ten miles from Hollywood. Southern California's climate and lifestyle were to his liking, but he couldn't find work that interested him. He spent a lot of time at the racetrack and in pool halls. By that year's end, he apparently had given up hope of finding employment. He had arranged

3

SUBTERRANEAN HOLLYWOOD

for his return to New Jersey when he at last found steady work. The job was as an office boy in the animation department at MGM Studios in nearby Culver City. It paid only thirty dollars a week, but it was more interesting and glamorous work than he could have found in Neptune, so he took an apartment by himself within walking distance of the studio and began his new life.

He liked the work but he was otherwise miserable. He had no social life and he was stranded in Culver City without a car. His only pastime was going to the two local movie theaters at night and on weekends. Neither changed its bill often enough to keep him occupied, though, and for the first time in his life he was lonely. "I'd never been anywhere where I didn't know everybody," he said. "I had no friends. It was only a couple of months, but it seemed like ninety years before I got to know some people."[2] Meanwhile, he grew despondent and worried about his future, questioning the wisdom of settling so far from home and friends.

Since he had no social life, Jack spent much time and effort winning friends at work. The studio personnel became his "town-folk," and he used his considerable charm to gain their attention and acquaintanceship; this, in turn, created opportunities.

One of his duties as an office boy was that of messenger; it gave him the run of the studio and the benefit of relatively unstructured time to get around and meet people. He used the opportunity to run a sports gambling pool, earning extra money while learning much about the behind-the-scenes business of moviemaking. It was a good position for an ambitious young man to hold. He made contacts in almost every department of the studio, contacts that could have gotten him into the production end of the industry had he chosen to work there. Such contacts were often more important in Hollywood than knowledge or talent.

Jack got to see movie stars at work, too. He had crushes on Grace Kelly and Rita Moreno, and he also admits that after he had worked there for a while and had begun to feel a part of the industry, he fantasized about being a movie star. But in light of June's bitter experience, he had no illusions. For all her beauty, talent, and show-business knowledge, she had failed to break into movies. Jack knew that the odds against his getting into motion pictures were greater than June's had been. He was not the tall, handsome type the studios were looking for then. He knew nothing about acting, either, and so never thought seriously about it. Besides, the industry was edging toward an economic recession by the time he began work at MGM. Television was wreaking havoc with the movie business, changing its structure, and moviegoers were staying home. Movie theaters were closing as television networks expanded across rural areas of the country. Veteran actors were drawing unemployment compensation because fewer movies were being made. The studios were phasing out the contract system whereby newcomers had been signed exclusively by the studios and trained to act, sing, and dance in films. Hundreds of studio-trained actors were being dropped from payrolls as their contracts expired. It was the worst of times to aspire to an acting career. Jack didn't; that is, not until the day he had words with one of MGM's veteran moviemakers.

The studio was a small town to Jack. He made a point of knowing every building and alleyway of it. He learned the names of studio executives, and while others avoided the moguls or treated them with reverence, Jack greeted them by their first names—and got away with it. It wasn't that he was a scheming Sammy Glick of the industry; for the most part, his familiarity was an extension of his small-town friendliness and natural inclination and need for establishing an intimacy with everyone he met. It was just such an encounter that made him consider an acting career. He is said to have passed producer Joseph Pasternak one day on the MGM lot. He had never met the executive, but he greeted him in his customarily familiar manner. Pasternak is alleged to have stopped him, looked him over, and said, "How'd you like to be in pictures?" The offer was genuine, and Jack accepted it. The producer arranged a screen test and sent Jack a scene from a script to study. It's been said that Jack didn't realize he was supposed to memorize his lines, and therefore failed the test. This is doubtful, since he had acted in high school plays and had been around the studio long enough to know what was required of him in a screen test. In any event, the test turned out badly and nothing more was said to him about being in pictures.

The experience would have been discouraging to an aspiring actor, but because Jack didn't have such aspirations, he was encouraged by it. The producer's interest apparently set him thinking seriously about acting. He presumably reasoned that if a professional of Joseph Pasternak's stature had seen something in him—some

17

potential as an actor—then perhaps he could develop that. Toward this end, he enlisted the aid of two friends in the animation department, cartoonists Bill Hanna and Joe Barbera. They used their influence with MGM's talent department to get him an apprenticeship at Hollywood's Players Ring Theater, which was the West Coast's most coveted showcase for young actors at the time. This led to his joining an acting class that changed his life.

The class was conducted by Jeff Corey. In it, young Nicholson found an intriguing world to explore—one that involved self-analysis and the practical application of psychology—providing him not only a purpose and direction but also a circle of friends from which he cultivated what he later called his "surrogate family." The class was the most intimate gathering he had encountered. Here was a group of individuals who, for their art, dropped their social masks and bared their deepest emotions, revealing sensitivities and vulnerabilities as only the closest of friends or family members dared do with one another. It was instant intimacy. For Jack, who longed for both intimacy and acceptance above all else, the class became family and the art a way of life.

Among the students in his class were then-unknown actors James Coburn and Sally Kellerman; writers Carol Eastman, Robert Towne, and John Shaner; and a young producer named Roger Corman. Under the pseudonym Adrien Joyce, Carol Eastman would later write the screenplay for three of Jack's films: *The Shooting, Five Easy Pieces,* and *The Fortune.* Towne would also write three: *The Last Detail, Chinatown,* and *The Two Jakes;* and Shaner would write *Goin' South.* Producer Roger Corman was never quite as close to Jack as the others, but he watched him develop as an actor and was one of the few who early on considered him capable of handling leading-man roles. Corman's early belief in him and his later practice of casting him in his low-budget films assured Jack's continued apprenticeship when other doors were closed to him.

Eastman, Towne, and Kellerman befriended Jack; they were kindred spirits. They encouraged and consoled one another and drew close, like family. Jack and Robert Towne took a bachelor apartment together in Hollywood for a while to share expenses. Carol Eastman was like a sister to Jack. She was studying acting at the time, but was the most shy and reclusive of the group. Jack encouraged the writing talent that she displayed. Sally Kellerman sought Jack's advice. They, too, were like brother and sister and brought out the child in each other. Sally would often sit on Jack's lap and tell him about problems with her love life. He'd listen sympathetically and offer brotherly advice. At the time, she was taken no more seriously as an actor or a person than was Jack, so they shared with each other not only their hopes but also their frustrations and disappointments. In weak moments, they went on food binges together. Usually, they binged on ice cream and potato chips, which in their playful, childlike intimacy they called "sweeties and souries." They have remained friends and have shared in each other's triumphs over critics who thought neither of them would amount to anything in motion pictures.

In early July of 1955, shortly after Jack turned eighteen and had been attending acting class only a few months, he got word that John Nicholson had been hospitalized in Neptune with a heart condition and cancer of the colon. The elder Nicholson died two weeks later of cardiac arrest.[3] Jack didn't go back for the funeral. Had he been older and more settled, or had he known the truth of his birth, he might have gone. He had strong feelings for John, but at the time they were more of pity than respect: John Nicholson had been the hapless alcoholic "father" who had done little more in that role than make his family's life more difficult. Jack felt no overpowering need, therefore, to pay his last respects or to see John laid to rest. Besides, Jack hated funerals, and attending John's would have been a hardship. "The financial aspects of the trip made it prohibitive," he said, "or at least gave me reason for it to be prohibitive. I didn't want to fly back East just to go to a funeral."[4] John was buried on July 26, 1955, at Mt. Calvary Cemetery in Neptune City.

Jack became more involved with the acting crowd in the following two years—not with the movie colony's glamorous elite but with what might be called its subterraneans, those whom the entrenched viewed with disdain as a nest of raucous and seemingly indolent heathens who had taken up camp outside studio walls. June wasn't pleased with this turn of events. She was even less pleased when Jack quit his job at MGM and later drew unemployment compensation while pursuing his new career. She no doubt hoped that he would mend his ways when his unemployment benefits were exhausted, but even then he managed to stay in acting class and to get along by hustling pool and gambling at the racetrack. In the meantime, he had formed a habit of staying out all night with the young aspiring actors and actresses, most of whom were decidedly nocturnal. He cruised the streets with them and made the rounds of coffeehouses and wine and pot parties, then slept away his mornings and early afternoons.

June was convinced that Jack was becoming a bum. He had his youth, charm, and intelligence; he also had the potential for doing something constructive with his life. However, she thought he could do so only if he applied himself in some worthwhile trade or profession. Acting? She knew the odds against anyone making a living at it. Had John Nicholson lived, he would have been amused by Jack's escapades, just as Shorty was, but June was more practical and she wasn't amused. She considered him totally irresponsible and his lifestyle reprehensible. She thought he was wasting his youth and, worse, drifting aimlessly, just as John Nicholson had done before him.

June had cause for alarm. She knew Jack well and saw that in those early days he was trying to become an actor not from a profound need or drive to express himself as an artist but from an attraction for the lifestyle and camaraderie of the would-be actors he had befriended. It was a lifestyle she considered bohemian, at best. After he became an established actor, Jack admitted that he had gone into acting only for, in his words, the "parties and people and girls and art and acceptance and all the things that are really very momentary and immediate."[5] June knew this and had many arguments with Jack about it. They fought and he lamented at how conservative she had grown over the years. He had found a life that suited him, and he had no intention of changing his ways.

As with his high school studies, Jack's interest in acting seemed more social than professional. To paraphrase his earlier comment about his studies, he wasn't really interested in acting at first. It seemed he was meeting the acting-class requirements only to enjoy what he liked most: being around a lot of people and having a good time. This was certainly the impression he gave others. He seemed nothing more than a small-town cutup who had drifted into Hollywood during the period of its upheaval and who was running around, wide-eyed and fascinated with subterranean Hollywood's carnival-like atmosphere and by the swirl of sideshow people it was attracting. There were strange and talented young actors like James Dean and Marlon Brando, both of whom were in town and working hard at the time; there were the Dean and Brando emulators, eccentric, brooding, and introspective young men (and those who only pretended to be those things); there were beautiful young women who were drawn to Hollywood by the lights, many of whom were by inclination more aggressive and uninhibited than their counterparts in other walks of life—inclinations that young Nicholson, who had a large libido, eagerly exploited; and there were painters, poets, sculptors, musicians and folksingers, and philosophical types—camp followers of Sartre, Camus, Kierkegaard, and of their own generation's explorer of internal roads, Jack Kerouac. Jack Nicholson wandered among them, astonished and sometimes repelled but ever intrigued and stimulated by the often bizarre goings-on.

This subterranean subculture was the antithesis of the once-glamorous movie colony, and Jack has become one of its most illustrious products. He is not one of those humanoid stars that were manufactured on the studio assembly lines once upon a time; his stardom rose from Hollywood's rubble—an unlikely ascent, and one that can be understood only in its own context. The times themselves tell a good deal about Jack Nicholson, for he is as much a product of the subterranean subculture as the old-time stars were of the studio system.

What characterized subterranean Hollywood in the late 1950s was its own faddish adaptation of a small but artistically influenced countercultural movement of the day, the Beat Generation; it was a movement that had spread from its spawning grounds in New York City's Greenwich Village and San Francisco's North Beach. At its purest, it was an existential artistic renaissance of sorts, a reaction to the increasing collectivity of modern life, with its ever-present threat of collective death, and a reaffirmation of the individual's supremacy in society. At its base was the conviction that the sanctity of the individual, and of individual freedom as the foundation of all moral and social freedoms, had been breached and that, as a result, the increasingly complex and collective world society was plunging, like lemmings, into a valueless abyss.

The beatniks, as the movement's adherents were called, were driven by the notion that it was not *how* man lived but *why*. They were convinced that only through the restoration of the sanctity and dignity of the individual and his unfettered freedom to express himself could life again become meaningful and the joy of it celebrated. Author Lawrence Lipton called the beatniks "holy barbarians," and rightly so, for in essence theirs was a search for the "holy I," a time of self-examination, of self-expression, and, in its extremes, of seemingly wild and hedonistic self-indulgence. It was a movement after Jack's own heart, and he burrowed into the belly—if not the heart—of this developing subculture and was truly content. He didn't grow a beard and wear sandals or go barefoot and carry a guitar slung across his back (as did his friend Warren Beatty, for example), but he was notably susceptible to its hedonistic excesses and attuned to much of its antiestablishment philosophy.

The word *beat* was coined to express the generation's state of spiritual bankruptcy—the emptiness of it, the beatness of it. The Beats rejected establishment mores, exalted individual freedom and its expression above all else, and studied philosophies such as Zen Buddhism and other exotic forms of Oriental mysticism. Unfettered self-expression was their benison, and the arts their realm; their voice was found in poetry (the distillation of subjectivism) and jazz—the latter because it was improvisational, the free expression of the creative individual rather than the interpretive group.

In Hollywood, the movement's emphasis was naturally on drama. It found expression in a hybrid of the Stanislavsky acting method that came to be called simply "the Method" and that Jack and most aspiring actors of the day adopted. The Method is to drama what jazz is to music. It, too, is an intensely subjective improvisational form of expression, one that entails the psychological analysis of the character to be portrayed (finding the heart, essence, or soul of the character) and then dredging up and utilizing corresponding emotions from the actor's own real-life experiences in the portrayal. The Method was advocated as a technique for reaching that plateau where the purest form of acting is done, for treading that precarious edge between reality and fantasy, an edge that is analogous to and as treacherous as the thin line between genius and insanity. This technique came to be formalized, named, and taught at New York City's Actors Studio, which is often credited with its discovery; in fact, it's a technique that extraordinary actors discover naturally for themselves and that had been undoubtedly in use from drama's very beginnings.

There were subtle and serious prerequisites to an aspiring actor's developing a technique that necessitated drawing from the well of personal experience. One was the necessity of having a sufficiently deep well to draw from. Many of the Method aficionados believed that one must have suffered to be properly prepared for the range of roles one might be called upon to portray as artist—as opposed to the mere technique needed to be simply a performer. It was believed that an uneventful middle-class upbringing was a handicap, so many of the young and inexperienced actors who adopted the Method used the pursuit of its development as license for self-indulgent behavior and to engage in wild and often bizarre activities solely for experience. This, too, contributed to the intriguing side-show atmosphere that young Jack Nicholson found in Hollywood.

Another prerequisite of the Method's adaptation was getting in touch with one's feelings—particularly those stirred by life's more traumatic moments—in order to reexperience and express them through one's art. Such feelings were often buried deep in the subconscious, and so the use of milder narcotics like marijuana were experimented with—not to escape the outside world, but to explore the world within, beyond the reaches of the conscious mind. Marijuana proved relatively useless for this purpose—counterproductive, in fact—but Jack was introduced to its use in 1957 when it was thought by some to heighten awareness. And he has never stopped using it. When he gained a measure of celebrity more than a decade later, he publicly admitted using marijuana and to have continued its use ever since. He also advocated its legalization. Later, he came to regret his public advocacy, not from moral considerations, but from irritation that his candid remarks about the drug were found by the show-business media to make more interesting copy than his acting or his films.

If tapping the subconscious freed the mind's creative powers of restraint and made one a better artist, then it was apparent to some that being a little crazy—a little neurotic if not psychotic—helped, too. Surely those with crazy streaks were living closer to the edge than were relatively well-adjusted people. Those who were touched with insanity sometimes compulsively acted out their traumas and

23

obsessions, oblivious to the fear of rejection or ridicule that restrained many actors. One had only to observe the tortured obsessive-compulsive gyrations of a talented actor like James Dean—on and off screen—to appreciate the raw, explosive power generated when one gave one's all for art by skirting the edge so boldly and unselfconsciously that one risked crossing over the abyss to that place that consumes one. Thus it became fashionable in subterranean Hollywood to be a little crazy, too.

There were genuine crazies, of course. Some managed to keep their balance on the edge; others didn't. There was the young actor who, shortly after James Dean's fatal auto accident in 1955, so wanted to be like his dead idol that he bought a Porsche and a red racing jacket like Dean's and drove off a cliff on Mulholland Drive. Mostly, though, the Dean emulators only feigned craziness. Author John Gilmore, himself a former actor, recalled an acquaintance of his and Jack's who used to do what were called "numbers"—senseless and sometimes outrageous acts—to prove how crazy he was. The actor did his numbers at private gatherings or in restaurants or other public places whenever he had an audience of his peers. Once, for example, while at a party attended by both Gilmore and Nicholson, the actor urinated against the host's kitchen wall. The actor and Gilmore and Jack used to get together at Gilmore's apartment on occasion. They'd drink red mountain wine, and the actor, who was always stoned, would roll one of his cigar-sized reefers, as they were called then, and would smoke it and rave about how mentally ill he was.

24

"He was under contract to Warner Brothers when Dean was there," Gilmore said. "He was serious about acting and had done some interesting work in pictures, but he was very much influenced by Jimmy Dean—doing numbers in an effort to emulate Dean's genuine emotional distress—playing the eccentric or crazy artist. So we'd have some wine, and Jack and I would listen to the actor chuckle and chortle about how much money he was costing Warner Brothers with his (chuckle, chuckle) misbehavior. I had heard it all before, of course, but Jack hadn't, and the actor was trying to impress Jack, who was really only a very new and casual acquaintance of ours at the time. The actor was looking for admiration, applause, and Jack wasn't applauding; he didn't say anything about the actor's ravings, but he shot me looks, as if to say, 'Just incredible!

Actors are begging for work, and this guy's trying to commit professional suicide!' "[6]

Jack would later do small numbers himself. He claims that a bit he did in *Five Easy Pieces*—the one where his character explodes with rage in a restaurant and clears the table of dishes, glasses, silverware, and food, sending them crashing to the floor—was based on his own action of an earlier time at Pupi's, a Sunset Strip coffee shop. Jack also has received interviewers at home while dressed in his bathrobe and wearing a baseball cap and plastic vampire teeth—numbers calculated to orchestrate the interviews, to keep them light and superficial, for he has worked to establish and maintain a mystique that he feels is vital to his stardom. He has always refused to do television talk shows, not only because he sees television as a threat to his livelihood but also because he fears revealing too much of himself to the public, and he usually grants print-media interviews only when he has a new film to promote.

The Beat movement in subterranean Hollywood, with its emphasis on Method acting, was influenced greatly by young actors who trekked between New York City and Hollywood following the ebb and flow of what they called "pure" work, meaning serious dramatic presentations not only in legitimate theater but also in live television—*Playhouse 90*, the *Kraft Theatre*, dramatic programs sponsored by U.S. Steel, Alcoa Aluminum, and the like. By the late 1950s, the television programs that once had been presented live from New York were being filmed at the Hollywood studios, and young actors who were not committed totally to the legitimate stage and who were having difficulty finding work in New York migrated west. Some continued to genuflect east, toward the Actors Studio, and most brought with them a snobbery toward the likes of Jack Nicholson, who seemed a dallying local to them, one who was content to remain in Hollywood and to take anything offered him in the way of TV or movie work, no matter how trashy. The New Yorkers were—or at least thought themselves—the pacesetters in Hollywood's new subculture, considering themselves serious (if not anointed) artists, and Jack simply didn't measure up to their procrustean standards.

Despite the intensity of the times and the frenetic activity in Hollywood, Jack stayed on the fringes, more a spectator than a participant. He always seemed to be along just for the ride, for the

25

fun of it, more interested in becoming a star than an actor. He seemed the kind whose apparent "dallying with form" the French writer-actor Antonin Artaud found "hellish and accursed." It appeared that Jack would not or could not commit himself totally to his art, would not risk the possibility of rejection that such a commitment entailed. Therefore, it was thought that he would never be, as Artaud insisted of the committed artist, like a victim, burning at the stake and signaling through the flames. It seemed to others that Jack would flash his killer smile and dance nimbly *behind* the flames, giving from certain perspectives the illusion of commitment, moving always from the center, though, backing from the heat of it but staying close enough to share its warmth without obligation. In effect, he gave the impression of being no different from the young man Lorraine had counseled a few years earlier to leave Neptune: Now he was hanging around subterranean Hollywood, where life seemed kind of easy for him and where everyone knew him and he was still, in effect, Jackie Nicholson. Small wonder that he was taken no more seriously by his Hollywood peers than by those back in Neptune.

Jack had a reputation for being one of those guys who are always around. Those who knew him then remember him as being pleasant, but quiet and detached. To some, he seemed frequently stoned on marijuana; indeed, there were few in the young acting crowd who smoked it more than he. And to some he seemed a little spacy even when he wasn't stoned.

He was rarely seen at casting calls or auditions, but he was a fixture at the young actors' nighttime haunts. Hollywood's first beatnik coffeehouse opened on Sunset Strip in 1957. It was called the Unicorn, and Jack was among its regulars. The place had an upstairs bookshop that catered to those with a philosophical bent and an outside patio with candle-lit tables in hidden nooks and corners, where dope was smoked. Satirist Lenny Bruce performed at the Unicorn, and it became one of the main hangouts for the young acting crowd. Other beatnik places were established owing to the Unicorn's success. There was the Renaissance, the Sea Witch, and Chez Paulette, all on Sunset Strip. It was at Chez Paulette where a young, easygoing Jack Nicholson narrowly escaped getting punched by a young tough he had gotten into an argument with one evening. Actor Robert Blake stepped between them before the hood could carry out his threat.

Another place Jack frequented was Cosmo Alley, a coffeehouse fancier than the Unicorn that was located on the little alleylike street that runs behind the Ivar Theatre between Hollywood Boulevard and Selma. Marlon Brando was dating one of the waitresses who worked there, and Jack went there chiefly to catch glimpses of Brando, who was his idol in those days.

Jack's favorite hangout was the Raincheck Room on Sunset Boulevard (still open today), which is a few doors down from the spot where L.A.'s most important Off-Broadway–type theater, the Players Ring, used to be. The Raincheck Room was a bar that served a good steak sandwich and salad and where the young actors could gather and talk without being hassled and rustled from their tables in favor of better-paying customers. Jack was a regular there even though he didn't drink much. He never had held liquor well, which he demonstrated one night at the Ash Grove, a fancy and popular folksinger joint on Melrose Avenue.

Jack, John Gilmore, and cowboy-folksinger Jack Elliot spent an evening drinking and listening to music at the Ash Grove. When they were ready to leave, Jack got to his feet and realized that he was too drunk to walk. He managed to stagger out of the club, but once outside, he vomited on the sidewalk and then lay facedown on the grass between the sidewalk and curb, unable to get up. Under the influence themselves, Gilmore and Elliot tried to coax him to his feet, but he just lay there, motionless, almost unconscious. They finally helped him up and propped him against one of the iron poles that supported the Ash Grove's building-to-curb awning. Jack gripped the pole tightly, his knuckles going as white as his face. He could only nod, eyes tightly closed, when asked if he had a good grip on the pole.

His plight aroused the maternal instinct of one of the Ash Grove's waitresses, and she came out and helped him to Gilmore's car. Gilmore took him to a place on Sunset where he wanted to go and dropped him off. A week or two later, Gilmore saw him and Jack didn't even remember the incident. He usually drank in moderation. That night was a rare exception, and one of the few times he had lost his composure in public.

27

Young actors out on the town often gathered at the Unicorn until closing, then moved en masse to the Sea Witch, where late-night radio was broadcast live, and would wrap up the early morning at Canter's delicatessen on Fairfax, where, totally stoned by then, they would eat mountains of food. Few of them could afford many such nights, though. Usually, they would make the rounds of private bring-your-own-jug parties, where they would drink cheap red wine, smoke dope, and take turns playing bongo drums to jazz records. Later, when Jack rented a large house on the corner of Fountain and Gardner, it was party time at his place more often than not.

If there were no private parties going on or if the young crowd was bored, they often stopped by a private residence on Melrose Place where sex orgies were held. Most of the people who visited there were just spectators. There was always a lot of marijuana and liquor, and the orgies were accompanied by exotic Eastern or classical music played on a phonograph. The orgy participants often numbered about a dozen people who, as one observer put it, formed a big ball of sex on the living room couch and floor, seemingly oblivious to the presence of voyeurs who stopped by to have a drink and to watch the goings-on for a while before moving on to other places. It was usually the same dozen or so people who participated in the orgies; two of them have since become stars. Jack visited the place on Melrose often, but was never seen participating in the orgies. He would have had problems in those days even if tempted. He told *Playboy* that he suffered from a sexual dysfunction—premature ejaculation—until he was twenty-six or so, a condition that plagued him until he got into Reichian therapy in the early 1960s.[7] He has always been compulsively candid about such intimate personal details, which is another reason he shuns talk shows and grants few interviews.

Another place that the young acting crowd frequented on quiet nights was Samson DeBrier's. DeBrier was a movie aficionado whose house was an open salon of sorts, cluttered with studio movie props and with autographed photos of actors and actresses he had known. The reading of tarot cards was common at DeBrier's salon, though DeBrier himself seldom participated in the readings; more often than not, he sat in his kitchen, holding court there, and occasionally he'd stroll through the house to greet newcomers. Sometimes, too, he'd turn the lights low and read aloud from his memoirs, a practice that young Jack Nicholson found exotic.

It was at DeBrier's that Jack first saw James Dean in the spring of 1955, just months before Dean's death, and was snubbed by him. Dean and John Gilmore were friends from their days in New York City, and Gilmore took Dean to meet DeBrier one night when Jack happened to be there. Kenneth Anger's *Inauguration of the Pleasure Dome* had been filmed recently at DeBrier's house, featuring DeBrier, Anaïs Nin, Curtis Harrington, Paul Mathison, and others, and Dean was interested in the film and wanted to meet DeBrier.

Gilmore and Dean had gone to DeBrier's on their motorcycles. Somewhere that evening, they had picked up a young woman with one leg, who kept telling the story of how she had lost her leg to people at the party. Jack was all smiles, obviously pleased to see Dean arrive and eager to meet him. Gilmore introduced them, but Dean was not friendly; he mumbled something to Jack and turned his back to resume his conversation with DeBrier. Gilmore was embarrassed for Jack and made excuses. He explained that as they had been riding along, the wind had affected Dean's hearing and his eyes—which wasn't true. The snub had nothing to do with Jack personally; Dean was always self-absorbed and could be very rude.

Jack turned to the woman with one leg and listened to her story sympathetically. He didn't let on that he was bothered by Dean's action, but he never brought Dean up in conversation with Gilmore after that, though he was clearly interested in learning as much about him as he could. He would always raise the subject obliquely, Gilmore said, usually by discussing Dennis Hopper and the possibility of Dean's influence on him, thereby steering the conversation around to Dean without seeming to do so.

In late afternoon, Jack could usually be found at one of the daytime hangouts such as Barney's Beanery on Santa Monica Boulevard or Schwab's Pharmacy on the Strip. John Gilmore recalls seeing him at Schwab's often. As was the practice then, Gilmore would drop into Schwab's and meet with other actors on the restaurant side of the store, where they would discuss acting or motion pictures or filming techniques.

"Jack would wander in and sit down with us," Gilmore recalled, "and he'd just sit there, smiling and pleasant, but looking around

29

distracted, to see who was arriving or leaving the place and not really paying much attention to our conversation—just being there and yet not being there, too. This was an intense period for actors in Hollywood. A lot was happening. There were changes in the industry and in acting and directing and cinemagraphic techniques, and a lot of us were trying to do good work—serious work—and sharing experiences and ideas. Jack didn't seem at all interested or concerned with any of it. He was just hanging around, having fun, and so no one took him seriously as an actor."

Gilmore says that Jack seemed to lack intensity and that nothing appeared to bother him much, as though all was right with the world and he didn't have a care. "He always reminded me of a department store mannequin," Gilmore said. "It was as though someone would come in with this Jack Nicholson mannequin and set it down in the booth with us at Schwab's, and it would just sit there, smiling. If Jack came in with another actor, like Harry Dean Stanton, the other actor would join our conversation or follow it with interest, but not Jack. Occasionally, he'd do some bit or impression or he'd tell a joke that had nothing to do with what we were discussing, and we'd kind of laugh along with him to save him embarrassment. His jokes weren't funny; he had a peculiar sense of humor. Mostly, though, he'd just sit there, smiling. I mean, he'd say hello, but that was all. And if we were discussing something that we considered heavy about acting—something that should have interested anyone serious about acting—Jack would just disconnect. After a while he'd get up and wander off, disappear. I don't care who claims now to have seen potential in him, the fact is no one took him seriously then. He was just a pleasant guy who hung around and who eventually took any terrible acting role offered him, stuff that most of us had turned down as garbage and that we thought unfit to screen, let alone work in."

Gilmore did a lot of movie work and starred in television anthologies and on stage at the Players Ring, where he received excellent notices as the lead in William Inge's A Loss of Roses. He has admitted that there was a lot of snobbery among actors in those days, particularly among those who had worked and studied in New York City and were holding out for "pure" work while looking down their noses at anyone who seemed to be angling only for stardom

30

and money. "Ultimately, the laugh was on us," he says. "Most of us got neither the pure work nor the money."

Despite perceptions to the contrary, it wasn't all play for Jack. According to his own recollections, he was more serious about acting than most others realized or gave him credit for. He continued his acting classes and helped establish a little theater in an old storefront on Santa Monica Boulevard with a small group made up mostly of his fellow students. They called it The Store Theatre; Jack and some of its members built it mostly from stolen material. "We didn't have a penny," Jack said. "We used to go out and steal lumber from lumberyards at night. We stole toilets out of gas stations. Lighting, boards—everything we ripped off in one way or another. We spent a lot of time acting. That was really ripe learning. It was a time of freshness and discovery of what acting was all about, of meeting new people and being inspired by other people's work, of watching an actor or actress who could hardly talk come into class and then six months later suddenly do a brilliant scene. . . ."[8]

Among those who knew Jack during this period and who saw little evidence of the freshness and feelings of discovery and inspiration Jack recalled experiencing was his first drama coach, Jeff Corey. Corey told Jack that he saw no "poetry" in his work, and Jack is said to have replied, "Perhaps you're not seeing the poetry I'm showing you." In Corey's files there's a note about Jack that reads, "Consider terminating for lack of interest." And Jack says of this period, "Now, I was on fire at this point inside myself, but none of it was visible to anybody; it was all covered up with, you know, fake behavior."[9]

It was in 1957, three years after he moved to California, that Jack got his first break in motion pictures. The film was *The Cry Baby Killer*, produced by his former classmate Roger Corman. Corman had been producing his own films even before he entered Jeff Corey's class, which he joined to learn about acting from a producer's point of view and to make contacts among the better students, whom he could employ cheaply in his films. He had produced more than a half dozen motion pictures after leaving Corey's class, all low-budget, second-bill programmers made largely for teenage audiences, and even then he was beginning to focus on the summer drive-in market. Many of his 1960s films are considered campy or classics of high camp by some viewers today. This is particularly true of his quasihorror films, for he allowed a good deal of humor in them, sending up the very genre he was exploiting. At the time he signed Jack for *The Cry Baby Killer,* though, Corman was still developing a market and was dependent upon major distributors to release his product; therefore he was making fairly conventional genre films, mostly the science-fantasy horror kind with titles such as *Swamp Woman, The Undead,* and *Attack of the Crab Monsters.*

Jack's film debut in *The Cry Baby Killer* was not as a supporting player or extra, as would be expected, but as the film's star. He portrayed a seventeen-year-old named Jimmy Walker who is attacked by three teenage toughs at a drive-in restaurant while trying to regain the affection of his girlfriend, who had severed their relationship. During the attack, Jimmy picks up a pistol dropped by one of the toughs and fires it in self-defense, shooting two of his attackers. Thinking he had killed the two (neither, it turns out, was mortally wounded), he takes hostages and holes up in the restaurant storeroom. In the end, as police prepare to close in, Jimmy's girlfriend convinces him that he has killed no one, that she cares for him, and that he can plead self-defense, and so he surrenders.

Jack could be justifiably proud of his performance. A Marlon Brando influence is evident, but then almost every young actor of the day was influenced by Brando, consciously or not. Over all, it was a remarkable first effort, and one Los Angeles critic commented favorably on Jack's acting. Still, *The Cry Baby Killer* was shot in ten days at a reported cost of only seven thousand dollars; its lack of production values made the cost patently obvious, causing most critics to ignore the picture. It was a major event and accomplishment in Jack's life, of course. The fact that he made only a few hundred dollars as its star was relatively unimportant to him. What mattered was that he had *starred* in a motion picture, that it had been released by a major distributor (Allied Artists), and that he was at last a paid professional actor with a screen credit. It was an enormously encouraging beginning and one that Jack was confident he could build on. His career was launched—or so he thought.

To his dismay and bitter disappointment, it was two more years before he worked in another film—*The Little Shop of Horrors.* It, too, was a Roger Corman production. Rather than starring in it, Jack had only a bit part.

The setback was a shocking one. It wasn't in Jack's nature to wallow in self-pity, though; he disliked that in others and wouldn't tolerate it in himself. Though intimates such as Towne or Eastman may have had an inkling of his despair, he gave the appearance to others of being undaunted by the experience. He seemed the same old smiling Jack. Privately, he had his dark Irish moods, and this was the first of several low points in his career when, like the protagonist in one of his favorite short stories—Philip Roth's "Eli, the Fanatic"—he felt like taking refuge in his dark closet and lying on his shoes.

"I did all those
horror flicks
because they
were the only
jobs I could
get, man. No-
body wanted
me."

Jack Nicholson[1]

It was demoralizing to Jack that he was offered no film work for a long time after he finished *The Cry Baby Killer*. Matters looked gloomier still when, at about this time, he had a similarly disappointing experience following his professional stage debut as a supporting actor at the Players Ring Theater. In those days, television producers were hunting for new faces and new product to fill the hundreds of programming hours demanded each week by the viewers of the relatively new medium. They often signed actors right from the stage of the Players Ring. Jack knew this and hoped that his appearance would lead to work in television series.

The play was *Tea and Sympathy* and appearing in it with twenty-year-old Jack Nicholson were then unknowns Michael Landon, Edd Byrnes, and Robert Fuller. Jack wasn't singled out by critics

4

THE
PROFESSIONAL

for his work. He apparently acquitted himself well, though, and after the play's run he waited anxiously as one cast member after another was offered TV work. Jack was offered nothing. Other than experience, all he gained from starring in a motion picture and appearing in a successful play at the prestigious Players Ring Theater was a renewed eligibility for state unemployment compensation. As fellow cast members Landon, Byrnes, and Fuller went on to lucrative and steady employment as regulars in television series, Jack spent the Wednesdays of his next few months in line again with other out-of-work actors at the state department of employment.

For much of the entire following year, Jack went back to the same routine he had followed before his stage and screen debut. He resumed his party-time nightlife and spent his days going to occasional casting calls, his acting class, and the Hollywood Park racetrack, when the horses were running. He had always done fairly well betting at the track. He had won enough to buy his first car, a 1949 Studebaker. In time, though, his luck went bad and he stopped playing the horses. Losing money had little to do with his decision. It was losing, itself, that irritated him, and he eventually quit the track rather than subject himself to the agonizing frustration he suffered whenever he lost.

The doors to important producers remained closed to him, but he eventually found work doing occasional bit parts on live daytime dramatic television programs such as "Divorce Court" and "Matinee Theater." "Divorce Court" was the show he worked on most frequently, because it was loosely constructed and he was adept at improvisation. He portrayed a newspaper reporter on many segments of the show. Such work was neither steady nor professionally prestigious, but it kept him active as an actor and paid the bills. When he wasn't working, he maintained his movie contacts by visiting the sets and location shootings of friends who were. He often visited Corman's production company and helped out behind the camera, thereby working himself back in with that group.

In 1959, almost two years from the time he had done his first film, Jack began getting motion picture work again with small, independent producers. He worked on four films that year; all were released in 1960: *The Little Shop of Horrors, Too Soon to Love, Studs Lonigan,* and *The Wild Ride.* They were not important films, but they were useful to Jack because they gave him an opportunity to learn his craft and because people he met while making them were instrumental in getting him other work.

The Little Shop of Horrors was produced and directed by Roger Corman from an original screenplay by Charles B. Griffith. It was a send-up of horror films and concerned a man-eating plant and its bungling, naïve young owner's dilemma with keeping it fed. At one point in the film, the incredibly phony-looking plant ingests a gangster who has fallen into its foliage, and it makes appreciative chomping and slurping sounds before expelling the gangster's gun on the waft of a satisfied burp. And that was one of the film's more serious moments. Jack's appearance was brief but memorable. He did a funny bit part as a masochistic dental patient who refuses novocaine (because it "dulls the senses") and who squeals with delight under the drill wielded by a man posing as a dentist, registering alarm only when the man tries to stop drilling or refuses to pull a few of his good teeth. Though it got relatively little attention in its day, Little Shop has always been a favorite of film buffs—so much so that some twenty years later, in 1984, Warner Brothers reportedly paid Corman a half a million dollars for the remake rights to the film and then made a successful multimillion-dollar musical feature of it. The cost of Corman's original production was purportedly only $22,500.

Jack had a larger but secondary supporting role in Too Soon to Love, which was called a "now" film in its day because of its realistic portrayal of a serious sociological problem: an unmarried teenage couple's unwanted pregnancy and its social implications. Jack portrayed a friend of the young man who gets his girlfriend pregnant. The film was made by an independent producer and was released by Universal Studios. It made money and was lauded by a few critics for its serious intent, but it was nothing more than an artfully done B picture and was significant to Jack's career only in that its director, Richard Rush, was sufficiently impressed with Jack's acting to cast him later in two more pictures.

The production of Studs Lonigan was a relatively lavish one. The picture was based on novelist James T. Farrell's trilogy of the same name about a Chicago youth's disillusionment and untimely death in the 1920s. The film was directed by Irving Lerner and photographed under the supervision of Haskell Wexler, but it proved a box-office failure. For one thing, and much to Farrell's chagrin, it was given a Hollywood happy ending. But it failed mainly because the problems of adapting three novels to one feature-length film proved insurmountable. Jack had a small role as Weary Reilly, a member of Stud's youth gang. Critics praised the realism of the gang sequences, but young Nicholson's performance went unnoticed.

Jack's next film, The Wild Ride, was as low-budget as a B picture could be. It was released by Corman's Filmgroup, but it was partially funded by a northern California high school drama teacher. Jack played the lead as Johnny Varron, the ruthless and conceited hot rod–gang leader whose recklessness caused numerous automobile fatalities. Jack turned in a credible performance, despite the odds against his doing so. If nothing else, it proved that his instincts as an actor were good—that he could perform even without the guidance of a strong director. The film was notable for another reason: It was during the making of it that Jack got to know Monte Hellman, a young director who was working on the film as the associate producer. It was several years before Hellman and Jack worked together again, but Hellman came to exert a strong positive influence on Jack's career.

Jack's sixth film was The Broken Land, a preachy, pseudopsychological Western made by Lippert Productions. He played Will Broicous, the law-abiding son of a deceased gunfighter. The dialogue was so ineptly written that Jack's character spoke in the vernacular of a 1960s sociologist. The film was released in 1962 and was mercifully ignored.

After The Broken Land, Jack planned to go back to the legitimate stage as the lead in a West Coast presentation of Calder Willingham's play End as a Man. By this time—the summer of 1961—he had left Jeff Corey's class and had joined another, conducted by actor Martin Landau. The play was being cast from Landau's class, and Jack was set to play the part of Jocko when he was suddenly called to serve active duty in the armed forces.

Like many young men in those days of conscription, Jack was less than enthusiastic at the prospect of having to serve two years in the regular armed forces. To preclude that possibility, he had joined the Air National Guard years earlier and was serving in a reserve unit that demanded little of his time yet satisfied his military obligation. "That was a great rich kid's draft dodge," he said. "We were all draft dodgers; we didn't want to be in there. I started worrying about going into the army in about the fourth grade in New Jersey. I wasn't afraid of getting killed; I just didn't want to waste the time."[2]

Jack thought the reserves a perfect solution and never imagined that his guard unit would be called to active duty. But it was. Owing to unstable international developments caused by the disastrous Bay of Pigs invasion and, a few months later, the building of the Berlin Wall, his unit was activated and kept on alert from the summer of 1961 until the following summer. Jack spent the entire year stationed at the Air National Guard's Van Nuys, California, facility near Hollywood, where he was a fireman with an airfield crash crew.

There were moments during his year of service and his fire-fighting training that Jack found diverting. He was required to don an asbestos suit and be engulfed in flames, which he found "exhilarating." There weren't many such experiences to detract from the fact that his personal life and career were languishing while he spent a year in Van Nuys, however. This put him in the darkest of moods. He completed his time without incident, but he has suggested that his unit might have been better off without him, saying that he has a way of demoralizing people around him when he's trapped in such situations. Jack would have resented the encroachment on his freedom under any circumstances and would have reacted accordingly, but the interruption came at a time when there were new developments not only in his career but also in his personal life. He had fallen in love.

The woman was Sandra Knight.[3] She was an actress, and Jack had met her in Martin Landau's class a year or so before he was called to active duty. Sandra was a beautiful woman. Those who had known her before she met Jack—including an actor who dated her—considered her a nice, decent woman, charming and intelligent. Like Jack, Sandra had been struggling to establish an acting career. She attended acting classes and worked occasionally in daytime television, but she was neither obsessed with stardom nor

39

consumed with the need to perform, and in time she would give up acting.

Jack and Sandra began dating soon after they met in Landau's class. Shortly thereafter, Jack moved out of the place he had been sharing with another actor (probably Harry Dean Stanton) and into one with Sandra. They were very much in love, and on June 17, 1962, after Jack completed his military obligations, they were married in Hollywood by a Unitarian Universalist minister. Jack was twenty-five; Sandra was twenty-two. Harry Dean Stanton was best man at the ceremony.

Jack married, confident that he could get his career back on track after his year-long absence. He had arranged to do another Roger Corman film, *The Raven*, and it was at about this time—perhaps a little later—that he signed with the William Morris Agency. His agent there was a man named Sandy Bresler, who later formed his own agency and who has represented Jack ever since. Bresler was one of the few who thought Jack very talented, an opinion that probably wasn't shared by others in the agency. Bresler was undaunted by the opinions of others, though, and practically buried the agency in interoffice memos recommending Jack for almost every picture that was being cast.

By the time of Jack's marriage, Roger Corman had made a distribution deal with Sam Arkoff of American International Pictures. Corman had his own distribution company, The Filmgroup, but Arkoff and AIP had far better distribution and more money to invest, so they began backing some of Corman's more ambitious efforts. One of them was *The Raven*, a title (and nothing more) borrowed from Edgar Allan Poe. It was a typical Corman horror film, but AIP's backing enabled it to be launched as a comparatively classy production, with a screenplay by Richard Matheson, color cinematography by Floyd Crosby, and lavish gothic sets. The cast was also impressive—particularly to Jack, who had never worked with big-name veteran actors before. It included Vincent Price, Peter Lorre, and Boris Karloff. Jack had a feature role as Lorre's son, Rexford Bedlow, and it was without doubt one of the most interesting shootings with which he had been involved. The larger budget didn't affect Corman's style in handling the genre. It was an entertaining send-up, and its tone was exemplified by a scene in which Boris Karloff, portraying a magician who's searching for

40

his missing wife, asks the raven where she is, and the raven replies, "How the hell should I know?"

The picture was completed two days ahead of schedule, which meant that the rent was still paid on the soundstage and the sets remained standing. Corman took advantage of the opportunity by using the sets and soundstage to shoot the interiors for another picture. Boris Karloff was still available, as was Jack, and so it happened that young Jack Nicholson costarred with the great Boris Karloff in a horror film that was eventually released as *The Terror*. Corman didn't even have a complete script when he started the picture; he had only enough pages for two day's shooting, and when that was done, he closed the production down.

The harried two-day shoot without a script and on a soundstage that was about to be closed was the smoothest and easiest part of the production. The problem was that the footage shot for *The Terror* had been done with a union crew—the one that had shot *The Raven*—and Corman couldn't afford to pay union scale to complete the picture. It had to be finished cheaply with nonunion personnel and since Corman was himself a member of the Directors Guild—which forbade its members from working on nonunion productions—he couldn't even finish directing his own picture. He had to hire nonunion directors.

Like any small, independent producer, Roger Corman often had cash-flow problems and frequently had to rely on friends who would work on partial or deferred payment. This was presumably the case with the making of *The Terror*, for it was put together **41** piecemeal by several directors in the following weeks. Francis Ford Coppola directed for three or four days; Monte Hellman directed for three; then Jack Hale and Dennis Jacob each directed for a day or so. "Finally," Corman said, "at the end of it, there was still one day left to finish, and by that time I had run out of friends of mine who were directors and who'd come around for a day, and Jack said, 'Well, I'm as good as these guys; I'll direct it.' So Jack directed himself on the final day of shooting, and we put the picture together."[4]

It complicated matters to use several directors; each brought a unique interpretation to the story line and each tended to take the plot down a slightly different avenue, if not an altogether different direction. Corman credited Jack with giving the film whatever continuity it had, for as the film's main lead, a Napoleonic officer, he had scenes throughout and his work helped to coordinate them.

Jack's wife, Sandra, also had a role in the film, as Helene, the apparition of Boris Karloff's wife. It was the only time she and Jack worked together; indeed, it is thought to be her last appearance as an actress, for she quit the profession shortly afterward. Jack appeared more comfortable in *The Terror* than he had in *The Raven*, which is understandable given the fact that his role in the latter had been a secondary one and he had been called upon for the first time to do scenes with veteran actors—an intimidating experience. Both films made money, but neither was exceptional enough to draw critical attention. *The Terror* can often be seen on late-night television—particularly on cable TV, where it has become a late-night staple.

The year 1963 was memorable for Jack. *The Terror* and *The Raven* were released that year, marking his first appearance in pictures with established stars—a thrill for a young actor, despite the fact that the careers of two of the stars had waned. It was this year, too, that *Thunder Island* was released; Jack and Don Devlin had written the screenplay, and one critic said that although the film was flawed, the screenplay was better than average for a B picture. The release of *The Terror* also marked the first appearance of scenes Nicholson had directed. He didn't get screen credit for the directing, but he had in effect become an actor-writer-director that year—on a modest scale, to be sure, but anyone who has tried breaking into even one of those disciplines in Hollywood knows that to do so, modestly or not, is an extraordinary accomplishment. For the young man from New Jersey who had gone west to Hollywood just nine years earlier, it must have been encouraging and satisfying.

It was also in 1963 that Jack worked in his first major studio production. The film was *Ensign Pulver*, which was released by Warner Brothers the following year. It was a sequel to the successful *Mr. Roberts* and was directed by Joshua Logan. The stars were Robert Walker, Jr., Burl Ives, and Walter Matthau, and it was filmed on location in the waters off Acapulco, Mexico. Jack had only a small, unbilled part in the film as a sailor named Dolan. The picture failed, but the project had been worthwhile for Jack. He had gotten to watch a major motion-picture company in action; he had gotten several weeks' work with good pay; and it was his first trip outside the United States. Had he been able to make the shoot with an untroubled mind, it would have seemed like a paid vacation. The worst tragedy of his life had unfolded at home, however, and he had been troubled by it throughout the shoot.

> "There are two
> ways up the
> ladder: hand
> over hand, and
> scratching and
> clawing. It sure
> has been tough
> on my nails."
>
> *Jack Nicholson*[1]

There were two events in Jack's personal life in 1963 that by contrast couldn't have been more emotionally wrenching: the birth of his only child by Sandra—a daughter, whom they named Jennifer—and the sudden illness and death of June Nicholson, who died of cancer at Cedars of Lebanon Hospital, presumably in the fall of that year. Her death had troubled Jack greatly during the filming of *Ensign Pulver*.[2] Jack still thought at the time of June's death that she was his sister, but it's doubtful that knowledge of her true relationship to him could have made an appreciable difference in his reaction to losing her. He couldn't have adored her more, nor have been more grief-stricken. He had felt closer to June than to anyone. He had always felt particularly drawn to her, had always sensed that he was more like her than anyone else in the family.

5

TROUBLED YEARS

She was dying at Cedars of Lebanon Hospital when Jack was preparing to leave for the *Ensign Pulver* shooting in Mexico. "She looked me right in the eye," Jack said, "and said, 'Shall I wait?' In other words, 'Shall I try to fight this through?' And I said no."[3] June died the day he left for Mexico—while he was en route.

June kept her secret about Jack's birth even as she lay dying. "It didn't do her any good not to tell me," Jack said, "but she didn't because you never know how I would have reacted when I was younger. . . . Those women [June and Ethel May] gave me the gift of life."[4]

After Jack learned of his parentage years later, he changed his stand on abortion. He now states he is against it, saying that he doesn't have a right to any other view, even though this is contrary to his usually liberal bent regarding the sanctity of personal rights.

Jennifer was born the day Jack returned from Mexico. With a child to support and with his career at a seeming standstill, Jack again turned to screenwriting. This time, he collaborated with Monte Hellman, with whom he had worked several years earlier on *The Wild Ride* and who had directed him for a few days in *The Terror*. Hellman was five years older than Jack. He was a graduate of Stanford University and had done postgraduate work at UCLA's film school. It was while directing a legitimate play in Los Angeles that Hellman came to Corman's attention. Since first meeting Jack, Hellman had gained a reputation among independent producers as a director who could bring in a picture on time and within budget.

Jack and Hellman set out to write an exploitation film for Corman, one that would have sex and other commercial elements for the B market. They were convinced that such a film did not need to be cliché-ridden, inane, or badly written to be commercial. If they included the required elements, they believed that the B-market purveyors wouldn't care—or even notice—that the film also had something to say and said it well.

They titled the screenplay *Epitaph*. It concerned the life of a young actor on Hollywood's fringe, and it was semiautobiographical. The idea was that Jack would star in it and that it would include footage from his earlier Corman films. The script appeared to owe its philosophical thrust, if not its premise, to Albert Camus's essay *The Myth of Sisyphus*, at least that part of the treatise having to do with the irrationality of life and the absurdity of one's confrontation with it. The script also concerned the concept of the actor as hero, living life to the fullest by, in effect, living many lives through dramatic portrayals. This concept is noteworthy because it seems to have had a seminal influence on Jack's own philosophy; it's a theme that he has returned to in his other screenwriting efforts and that has apparently influenced his choice of roles since becoming a star.

Jack and Hellman took the script of *Epitaph* to Roger Corman. He showed interest in producing it, but before a deal could be made, Hellman was hired by another production company to direct two pictures to be produced by Fred Roos and shot in the Philippines. It was presumably through Hellman's influence that Roos hired Jack, who was given a major role in each picture and was commissioned to write the screenplay for one of them, *Flight to Fury*.

The first of the two films they did was *Back Door to Hell*, a World War II story about a three-man reconnaissance team (played by Jack, Jimmie Rodgers, and John Hackett) who land in the Philippine Islands prior to the American invasion and are drawn into battle beside a Philippine guerrilla unit they have contacted. It was a well-staged film, with good action scenes, but the script was so badly written and so replete with incongruous antiwar moralizing that it was destined to be just another bad war movie.

Their second picture, *Flight to Fury*, was written by Jack from a story by Hellman and the film's producer, Fred Roos. It concerns a psychopathic killer's murderous quest for a pouch of smuggled diamonds. In the end, no one gets the diamonds, and the psychopath, trapped in the jungle, takes his own life—and takes pleasure in that final, brutal act, as well. Jack wrote the part of the psychopath for himself and played it with enthusiasm. Monte Hellman thought it one of his most subtle performances. Certainly Jack was pleased with the character and the way he played it, but overall it wasn't a good film, and it apparently languished on the shelf for two years before it was sold to television.

Upon their return from the Philippines in late 1964, Jack and Hellman had lunch with Roger Corman to discuss their *Epitaph* screenplay. By then, Corman had decided not to do the film. He thought it too downbeat and esoteric for his market, and suggested that they do a Western instead. When they agreed and figured the

47

budget at only $75,000, Corman had them do a second Western while they were at it.

They set up a production office and Jack wrote one of the Westerns, *Ride in the Whirlwind*, while the other was contracted to his former acting-class friend Carol Eastman, who had submitted a scenario titled *The Shooting*. She wrote this under her pseudonym, Adrien Joyce. Jack is said to have done some writing on Eastman's script, too—presumably on the dialogue. He pored over diaries of the Old West in preparation for writing his own script, looking generally at language usage of the day and specifically for speech patterns and idiomatic expressions to give his dialogue the flavor of authenticity. This was probably in reaction to the experience he suffered earlier in the making of his Western *The Broken Land*, in which he was called upon to deliver credibly such lines as (with regard to his 1890s surroundings) "This sure is a lousy atmosphere."

Both scripts were finished by February 1965, and Hellman and Jack spent the next three months casting the parts, hiring a crew, working out logistics, scouting locations, and working on the countless details involved with the preproduction planing for a shoot. They began filming in May at a desert location near Kanab, Utah, working with only a skeleton crew of twelve (which included two wranglers, who cared for the livestock) and with very little equipment: a sound truck, an old station wagon, two cameras, and a few reflectors. What they lacked in numbers and equipment, they made up for in enthusiasm and esprit de corps, however.

The films were a labor of love for everyone, not only because the cast and crew were close friends and away from the prying eyes of the films' backers but also because they knew they were creating something that wouldn't be thrown on the screen as "giant apes and moaning carrots," to use Jack's phrase. They were producing something they thought extraordinary and worthwhile, and few of them had ever had such an opportunity. Hellman and Jack took care to give the films a naturalistic look and feel. The characters wore clothes authentic to the early West. The focus on them was economical and objective, revealing a people isolated in time and space. Their small existential dramas are played out against and dwarfed by a wasteland as foreboding as the circumstances that set them against one another. The characters did none of the things that would have been expected of them in a stereotypical Hollywood Western, which is exactly why the cast and crew approached the making of the films with inordinate enthusiasm and cooperation.

By July, both films were wrapped. Hellman, with Jack's help, spent the next six months editing them. The finished prints came out of the processing lab in January of 1966, a full year from the date the project was begun, and both films were then screened for Roger Corman. He was troubled by what he saw.

Neither film followed the traditional linear narrative that fans of Westerns had come to expect. Each was more a slice-of-life incident than a story, and each opened with very little exposition and ended without apparent resolution. Carol Eastman's script, *The Shooting*, opens with a former bounty hunter named Gashade (Warren Oates) returning to a mine he is working and finding another miner (Will Hutchins) badly shaken and nearly hysterical. Gashade learns that in his absence a third miner, his brother Coigne, has run off after running down a man and child with his horse in a nearby town. Into this scene steps a woman on foot (Millie Perkins). She buys a horse from Gashade and then hires him to escort her across the desert. She reveals neither her name nor her destination. Both miners accompany her, and in time another rider, whom Gashade suspects has been trailing them, joins the party. He is Billy Spear (Nicholson), a gunfighter. Spear takes Gashade's gun from him and eventually kills the second miner before Gashade jumps him and smashes his gun hand. Meanwhile, the woman has entered a canyon alone. Gashade runs after her and finds her raising her pistol and taking aim at his brother, Coigne, who is revealed to be Gashade's fraternal twin. Shots are heard. Both the woman and Gashade fall from apparently mortal gunshot wounds, Gashade calling out his brother's name as he falls. At this point, the film ends.

Jack's script for *Ride in the Whirlwind* concerns three cowboys —Wes (Nicholson), Vern (Cameron Mitchell), and Otis (Tom Filer)—who are returning from a cattle drive and accept the hospitality of strangers at an abandoned cabin, not knowing that they're outlaws. When a posse of lynch-prone vigilantes closes in on the group, the cowboys are mistaken for members of the

49

gang. Otis is killed, but Wes and Vern escape, taking refuge at a bleak homestead occupied by an old couple and their daughter (Millie Perkins). Eventually, Vern is killed and Wes kills the homesteader in self-defense before riding off alone, which is where the film ends.

Corman reportedly appreciated the artistry of both films but considered neither suitably commercial for his market. He decided not to invest the additional money needed to print and distribute them. Instead, he tried to interest larger distributors in them, even cutting the prologue from *The Shooting* to do so, but he could find no takers. He eventually sold his interest in the films very cheaply to another producer, who in time also decided that they weren't right for the market and who sold the American television rights to recoup some of his losses. (Monte Hellman later bought back the TV rights before the pictures were ever shown.)

Five years later, another producer-director, Jack T. Harris, bought the American theatrical rights to both films and tried to capitalize on Jack's rising stardom. He opened the films in a Dallas, Texas, theater a week after Jack was nominated for an Academy Award for his work in *Five Easy Pieces*, which was playing a hold-over run in Dallas at the time. Harris was confident that he could do business in Texas with two Westerns starring the newly nominated Jack Nicholson, but they drew no audience and no critical attention, closing in a week. Few Americans ever saw theatrical showings of the Westerns; they were shown only in Los Angeles and Dallas.

In a sense, Hellman and Jack violated the trust Roger Corman had placed in them. Their Westerns were no more commercial than *Epitaph* would have been, which Corman had turned down. It's said that Corman was too busy to read the Western scripts when they were completed and told Hellman to go ahead with the production, obviously trusting the director's judgment. After all, Jack and Hellman had been through the Corman "school" and knew what he wanted. Years later, both intimated that indeed they had known exactly what Corman expected of them. Hellman said that neither he nor Jack thought that anyone of importance would see the pictures. "We thought they would be a couple more Roger Corman movies that would play on the second half of a double-bill somewhere," he said, "so any thoughts about doing something different were for our own personal satisfaction."[5]

Jack was even more specific: "Roger [Corman] wanted some good tomahawk numbers with plenty of ketchup, but Monte and I were into these films on another level. . . . We thought of *Ride in the Whirlwind* as a kind of translation of *The Myth of Sisyphus*, the Camus essay where man's only dignity is in his return down the mountain after pushing up the stone. That's what our film was about: three guys returning from a cattle drive getting mixed up in some fracas."[6]

While Corman tried in vain to peddle the distribution rights in the United States, Jack took prints of the films to Europe—a trip presumably sponsored by Corman—where he entered them in film festivals, including those at Cannes and Edinburgh. The object was to interest foreign distributors. The films were well received, especially at Cannes, where they came to the attention of director Jean-Luc Godard. Because of Godard's influence, his endorsement of the films opened many doors for Jack. Even so, the distributor who finally licensed the French rights promptly went bankrupt. It was another year before the films opened in Paris, where they did fairly well.

Although the films were a commercial failure, they were milestones in Jack's career. Together with the two pictures he did with Hellman in the Philippines, Jack received invaluable experience in all phases of filmmaking, and the experience kindled his interest in writing and directing. These interests seemed to hold more promise for him at the time than acting and they were ultimately instrumental in his stardom.

51

After Jack returned from Europe, director Richard Rush offered him a part in a picture he was casting. Rush hadn't worked with Jack since 1959 in *Too Soon to Love*, but he remembered Jack's work in that picture and since that time had seen him do scenes at the West Coast Actors Studio, which Jack had joined after Martin Landau's class disbanded. The picture was *Hell's Angels on Wheels*. In it, Jack played the part of Poet, a young gas-station attendant who on impulse quits his job in order to experience the adventure and romance of the open road with a Hell's Angels motorcycle gang. However, Poet finds too much adventure (including senseless killings) and too little romance to suit him. The film differed from the motorcycle genre that had developed after the success of Marlon Brando's *The Wild One* in that it was the only one to use real Hell's Angels in the cast. The cast also included a young former model named Mimi Machu. She was to become Jack's leading lady in real life, for his marriage to Sandra was failing.

The topography of Jack's career in the late
1960s, like his moods, was one of inconsequential peaks and colossal depressions. A dozen
years had passed; he had turned thirty and was
considered too old for stardom by Hollywood standards. He had appeared in fourteen films, had
coproduced two and had written three. But he was
still having to grub even for the exploitation films
that he found so professionally, financially, and
spiritually withering. He had been away from
home very often, had been off to Mexico and then
to the Philippines, and then had immersed himself
for a year in producing two Westerns, including
the two-month location shoot in Utah, followed
by the trip to Europe. There had been little time
for Sandra. Even when he was home, he was busy
searching for solid footing, working on projects by
day and writing at night, giving work his undi-

6

**ON THE
ROCKS**

vided attention and feeling unjustly intruded upon whenever Sandra broke his concentration with demands on his time, or complaints, or with even minor domestic problems. "I couldn't take the arguments," Jack said, "they bored me."[2] This put an added strain on the marriage.

Jack and Sandra's problems ultimately caused them to see an analyst together, an event that led directly to the total collapse of their marriage rather than helping them. Part of the analyst's treatment was the administration of the hallucinogen LSD, which alters one's perceptions. Jack's experience with the drug was enlightening (it was at this time that he reexperienced the impressions of his infancy), but Sandra's experience terrified her. "This therapist didn't really understand LSD," Jack said. "He had never taken it himself. He gave it to Sandra first, in connection with a five-hour therapeutic session, but he gave her the maximum dosage. At one point, she looked at me and saw a demon, a totally demonic figure. For whatever reason, either because it's true about me or because of her own grasping at something, it was pretty bad."[3]

Perhaps owing partly to her natural inclination and partly to her bad experience with the drug, Sandra turned to religion for solace. "She became stimulated in a mystical area," Jack said, "and I couldn't get with that. I didn't want to get caught in a situation where I was in competition with God, or something like that, and I felt that I would be and that I would do it myself, because I felt the strength of this new flow into [her] life."[4] Jack claims that he isn't at all religious. He says the only time he ever prayed was when, at Bruce Dern's suggestion, he took up long-distance running to keep in shape. He often prayed while running, yet he doesn't know why he did so.

Sandra was horrified when Jack continued to experiment with the drug. She finally ordered him from the house and told him not to return. Their divorce became final in 1968 and ended with mutual respect and without rancor. They remained friends. Sandra eventually moved to Hawaii with Jennifer, but as Jennifer grew up, she spent part of her summer vacations with her father.

Meanwhile, in January 1967, shortly after he completed *Hell's Angels on Wheels,* Jack went back to work on another low-budget motorcycle picture, *Rebel Rousers,* starring Cameron Mitchell, Bruce Dern, and Jack's pal Harry Dean Stanton. The film was produced and directed by Dern's manager, Martin Cohen; at Dern's suggestion, Jack was cast in a feature role as the film's villain. It was the first of four consecutive films Dern and Jack worked on together, and it marked the beginning of a long and continuing friendship.

Bruce Dern had been a member of the Actors Studio in New York City and had gone to Hollywood in the summer of 1961. He met Jack while visiting Martin Landau's acting class that summer. Shortly thereafter, Jack was called to active military duty, so Dern didn't see him again until the winter of 1966, when he was working on a Roger Corman motorcycle picture with Peter Fonda called *The Wild Angels*. "I wanted Jack in the picture [*Rebel Rousers*] to play the leader of the bad guys," Dern said. "It was a good part, so I got him. . . . He was starting to go through his separation and divorce then, and that was a very rough time for him and he needed the job, and that kind of gave us a common bond."[5] Like several of Jack's early films, *Rebel Rousers* had a very limited release in only a few cities.

Jack continued to write. He drew on elements from his own life and from his experiences with LSD to write *The Trip*, the story of a young television-commercial director facing a separation from his wife and disillusionment with the crass commercialism of his profession. The director takes LSD in an effort to see his life from a different perspective. Jack's idea was to tell the story from an objective, camera-eye view, to record the protagonist's reaction to the fantasies he experienced, and to suggest the fantasies with widely spaced jump cuts of fleeting images that were almost subliminal because of their split-second duration on the screen. He wrote a part for himself, that of John, the drug guru who guides the protagonist through his drug trip.

He took the script to Roger Corman, who was very impressed with it; indeed, everyone who read it thought it brilliantly written. Corman got financing from American International Pictures and cast Peter Fonda as the lead, Susan Strasberg as Fonda's wife, and Dennis Hopper in a dual role. Instead of giving Jack the part of the drug guru, however, Corman offered it to Bruce Dern, saying that he owed Dern a favor. This didn't set well with Jack, for Dern had become Corman's favorite after the producer came to believe —along with everyone else—that he had been wrong in trying to

55

cast Jack as a leading man. Jack resented Corman's action, but he didn't let it affect his friendship with either man.

Corman shot the picture in the early summer of 1967. It took him only three weeks, and in doing so he expanded many of Jack's jump-cut fantasy images to full-blown scenes. He did this in order to show the interior of the drug-taker's mind, a technique that Jack thought unwise. "It's like the exact thing you don't want to do when you put a novel on the screen," he said, "unless the fantasy has a scenario of its own. The images are much too specific to go as fantasy scenes."[6] Corman's changes didn't hurt the film appreciably, but then AIP began tampering with it.

Initially, AIP requested only a couple of minor changes, and they were made. Before the project was over, however, someone at the studio had second thoughts about releasing a drug-oriented film and had Corman make cuts that he and Jack thought harmful to it. Then, after Corman had made the required changes and had left for Europe on another project, AIP made more changes. "They cut several sections out that we thought important," Corman said. "They changed the ending in a slightly innocuous way. They put some sort of optical break across the film to imply that it had been a bad trip, and the break or crack would mean that the character's personality and his life were now cracked and destroyed, which was total nonsense. The original ending was to leave it open, to let the audience decide whether it had been a good or bad trip."[7]

The film attracted critical attention, as Jack thought it would. But coming at last to the attention of the nation's foremost movie critics as a screenwriter proved a bitter experience for him. The reviews were mixed. A few critics seemed mesmerized by the film and praised its composition and its "brilliant" depiction of the "abyss between reality and fantasy." The most prominent critics, however, were insulted by its incoherent inanity. Jack, too, hated the film as it was finally cut. It wasn't a good representation of the screenplay, and though he understood why some critics disliked the film, he resented the fact that they placed much of the blame on his screenplay. It was another not-so-subtle reminder for him that film is a collaborative medium and that actors and writers usually have little control over what is finally projected on the screen. His experience with The Trip convinced him more than ever that his place in the film business was behind the camera, as director.

The last film Jack did for Roger Corman was made in the fall of 1967. Corman made a deal with the Twentieth Century-Fox B unit to produce and direct *The St. Valentine's Day Massacre*, which was based on the infamous 1929 Chicago gangland slaying of six Bugs Moran gangsters by their Al Capone gang rivals. It was a moderately budgeted film with a good cast, including Jason Robards, Jr., George Segal, Ralph Meeker, Jean Hale, and Bruce Dern. Corman offered Jack a feature role as one of the Moran gang leaders, but Jack chose to play a bit part instead because he needed money; the larger role would have given him only a few day's work, but Corman structured the shooting so that Jack's bit-part character, a getaway driver named Gino, appeared in scenes shot in both the first and last weeks of the production. So by Guild rules, Jack was on the payroll during the entire shooting, which lasted six or seven weeks.

It was also during the fall of that year that Jack got a role in an exploitation film about the hippie drug culture in the Haight-Ashbury district of San Francisco, produced by Dick Clark's company. Jack had done a screenplay for them, but it had been turned down by AIP, who was supposed to have financed and distributed the picture. Director Richard Rush read Jack's script and wasn't surprised that it was rejected. "It was a very imaginative, somewhat esoteric, fairly brilliant piece of writing," Rush said. "It hardly qualified as an exploitation film in the genre as it was known then."[8] Rush was brought into the project after Jack's script had been turned down and another—titled *Psych-Out*—had been chosen instead. Jack had nothing to do with the writing of *Psych-Out*, but when Rush filmed it, he incorporated three scenes from Jack's script.

Susan Strasberg and Bruce Dern, who both had appeared in *The Trip*, were cast in the picture along with Jack, Dean Stockwell, Adam Roarke, Henry Jaglom (who would later direct Jack in *A Safe Place*), and Jack's girlfriend, Mimi Machu (as Pandora), who was billed as I. J. Jefferson. Jack portrayed a rock musician named Stony in the film. It was a feature role, but he didn't do it for the acting credit, just for the money. His interest had been solely in doing the screenplay, because a writer could build on such credits and go on to better things, but an actor's role in such films led nowhere. He had done seventeen pictures as an actor by then, and he was totally unknown and broke. He wanted off the acting treadmill.

57

One day that winter, John Gilmore was driving to work when he saw Jack walking south on Wilcox near the Hollywood Boulevard intersection. Gilmore called to him, and Jack waved and smiled. When Gilmore pulled his car to the curb, Jack asked where he was going.[9]

"Down to Melrose," Gilmore replied.

"Me, too," Jack said. "I sure could use a lift."

Jack got into the car and told Gilmore that he had just left his car at a service station a block north; it was an old car, he said, and "screwed up." Everything was going wrong with it all at once. Gilmore thought Jack looked tired. "He was almost pale," he said, "and he seemed troubled. Those of us who had known Jack over the years had always thought of him as having had an easy life. He always seemed to have money and no cares, so I was surprised at his appearance and felt sorry for him. His shoes were scuffed up and worn down at the heels, and his jacket was in pretty bad shape. He had a beaten look about him, and he had been walking rather slowly along the street, some papers and what looked like other writing material under one arm.

"I asked him how the acting was going, and he just said 'Fuck!' Nothing more. He was quiet for a moment or two, then he said, 'It just hasn't worked.' "

"What hasn't worked?" Gilmore asked.

"I thought I was working for something, but it just hasn't come through," Jack said. "You wait for the tooth fairy—shit! You put the damn tooth there, and more than that, and she doesn't come. Everything's all fucked up, man."

"I saw the film you wrote for Corman, *The Trip*," Gilmore said.

"Fuck," Jack said again, this time more quietly and more from frustration than anger. "I want to write. I'm through with acting. I don't want to do it anymore, man. Parts are shittier and pictures are shittier and what's the point if you're not going to be able to bring something to it?"

Jack told Gilmore that he thought he had brought more to the writing of *The Trip* than he had to all the work he had done as an actor. He hated how the picture had turned out, but the writing of it had been creatively fulfilling.

By this time, Gilmore had given up acting and was working under contract as a project coordinator and screenwriter for Robert Levy's Pebble Productions, on Melrose Avenue near La Cienega, where he was writing scripts for Jean Seberg, among others. Gilmore suggested that Jack meet Levy; with Jack's screen credits, there was a chance that Levy might give him a contract to write or develop properties. Pebble was trying to put out what the trade papers had announced as "handcrafted movies," good low-budget films rather than the bad low-budget product that most small production companies had been grinding out solely for profit. Jack liked the idea and said he needed the money. He was broke. "He was having problems with his personal life," Gilmore said, "and he needed the shift, the change. He said it was something that he should have done before, but had kept after acting, had kept after it even though it had stopped doing anything for him."

Jack decided that meeting with Robert Levy might be a good idea, so Gilmore drove him to the production offices. They got take-out coffee at a nearby hot-dog stand and then went up to Gilmore's office to wait for Levy, who had been detained. They waited for a long time and talked. Jack was fascinated by a poster-size photograph in Gilmore's office of rock and roll star Janis Joplin, showing her with one breast exposed. The photograph was inscribed "To John, with love and kisses." Joplin had given it to Gilmore when he was in San Francisco working on a film project about the Berkeley campus riots. Jack was intrigued by Joplin and wanted to know every detail of Gilmore's encounter with her. "He asked me flat out if I'd screwed her," Gilmore said, "but I didn't comment on it. He said he'd really like to get together with her, but felt that she'd probably laugh at him because of the recent movies he had done on dope and on biking. He said she'd think they were 'jok-able.'"

Jack waited in Gilmore's office for nearly two hours, but when Levy didn't return, he left to catch a bus on Melrose. Gilmore felt at the time that Jack was at a point in his life where he had surrendered, where he was overcome with the realization that he couldn't or wouldn't make it as an actor, where he felt lost, left out. "I'm sure he was feeling his age," Gilmore said, "and how much longer could he continue making B pictures that no one noticed or cared about? He had tasted creativity in the writing; it had demonstrated that worlds beyond acting existed and were attainable. I thought Jack would come back to see Levy, but I didn't see him again until after he became a star."

The reason that Jack never returned to Pebble Productions was that shortly thereafter he found an extraordinary job with another small but well-financed production company, Raybert Productions, which had offices at Columbia Studios on Gower Street. Raybert had been formed by director Bob Rafelson and producer Bert Schneider, both former Universal Studio producers who had teamed up and had prospered marketing a quasi-pop-rock group called the Monkees. The Monkees were not a true musical group; they were a media creation developed expressly for television by Rafelson and another director, James Frawley, and fashioned loosely after the Beatles and other rock quartets of the day. The group was made up of two actors and two musicians, each chosen for his stereotypical likeness to what was perceived as constituting most rock groups: a tall, skinny character, a handsome one, a loony one, and a clownish one. In short, the Monkees were fashioned as a weird cross between the Beatles and the Marx Brothers, and their zany but simplistic situation-comedy television series, packaged by Columbia Pictures, was so popular—particularly with preteens—that Columbia's record division even recorded them. To almost everyone's surprise, many of their records became hits and the group's popularity skyrocketed. It was natural that Raybert and Columbia would capitalize on the group's success by featuring them in a full-length theatrical film—though Raybert's and Columbia's motives for doing so were widely divergent. It was while mulling over ideas for the film that Bob Rafelson met Jack Nicholson.

Rafelson and Jack liked each other immediately. Bob Rafelson was the kind of iconoclast that Jack admired but rarely encountered in the picture business. He had begun his career at the CBS Television Network in New York City, where he became story editor for David Susskind's prestigious dramatic television anthology *The Play of the Week*. From there, he went to Universal Pictures as an associate producer before teaming up with Bert Schneider. The manner by which Rafelson parted with Universal was in itself enough to win Jack's admiration; Rafelson is a big and physical man, and he's said to have left the studio after turning over his boss's desk during a heated argument.

Jack was astonished and intrigued when he learned what Rafelson had in mind for a film about the Monkees. Curly, as Jack nicknamed him (Rafelson was going bald), planned to expose the group as a phony, superficial media gimmick and to do so, apparently, with the group's cooperation by satirizing its success and inanity as a reflection of our disposable-plastic times. The picture was called *Head*, and Rafelson later said of it, "*Head* was never thought by me or my partner [Bert Schneider] as a picture that would make money. What we felt was that we were entitled—since we made Columbia an enormous amount of money in their record division and in TV sales—to make a picture that would in a sense expose the project."[10]

It was Jack's kind of project. Presumably, he was brought into it because of the experience and know-how he had gained as a co-producer and writer with Monte Hellman, for Rafelson hired him not only to collaborate with him on the script but also to coproduce the film. It seemed an extraordinary opportunity, but Jack was ambivalent; he looked upon the opportunity largely as a manner of working into a directorial position with Raybert. He was wary about the project itself; he had been burned before by getting too creative, enthusiastic, and optimistic about such projects—*The Trip*, for example—and he didn't want to set himself up for more emotional frustration. "I thought the guy was very honest, very open," he said later of his early days with Rafelson. "He blew my mind a few times. I said, 'Don't get me up to full creative amp. Let's write a fair movie and do the best we can. Don't cop out on me, because I won't like it; I'll be very upset.' And he never did. We made exactly the film we wanted to, an honest expression about a particular phenomenon: the suicide of the Monkees."[11]

The film was as surrealistic as the group itself. It starred the Monkees, with cameo appearances by Annette Funicello (as Minnie), Victor Mature (The Monkees were hired to portray the dandruff in his hair for a TV commercial in the film), Mimi Machu (as Lady Pleasure), and others, including brief appearances by Jack and Rafelson as themselves. The film was free-form and plotless, and occasionally caustically satirical, a fast-cutting series of impressions: the Monkees in concert; cut to Vietnam war footage; cut to the Monkees now in a war film; cut back to the concert scene, where the Monkees' preteen fans are tearing dummies of them to shreds; cut to a desert scene, where one of the group is preoccupied with getting either his money back or his soft drink from a malfunctioning Coca-Cola machine while remnants of the Italian army try to surrender to him; cut to one of the group looking into the camera lens and then fixing his eyes to a spot somewhere behind the camera (to an unseen Rafelson) and declaring, "Bob, I'm through with it!" and exiting right through a painted backdrop.

While *Head* marked the end of the Monkees' popularity, it didn't contribute to their demise. It was a box-office failure and wasn't seen by enough people to influence the group's popularity one way or another. The Monkees were on the wane even as Jack and Rafelson planned the film.

Some critics liked *Head*. All seemed to understand what Jack and Rafelson had been trying to say in it, but the majority—particularly the influential ones—questioned whether the message was worth the filmmakers' labors. Jack loved the film and didn't care what critics said of it—or at least didn't let what they said trouble him. By the time *Head* was released, he was engrossed with other matters, anyway. He had already begun preparing for a film he would eventually direct, and had been sidetracked against his wishes to do a bit part in another film, *Easy Rider*.

The irony was that Jack became a movie star
only after he had stopped trying to be one,
and that he looked upon his impending participation in *Easy Rider* as an obstacle and an im-
position.

He had played a small part in bringing the film
project to executive producer Bert Schneider's attention, but he wanted nothing else to do with
it. What he wanted was to be left alone with
another project he was developing, one that he
hoped would launch his career as a director. It
was presumably only as a favor to Bert Schneider
that he got involved with *Easy Rider,* and that
was after the cast had been chosen, the shooting
had begun, and after the project began showing
the stress marks of an impending disaster. It had
been a very wobbly and self-indulgent venture
from the beginning.

7

THROUGH
THE
LOOKING
GLASS

The project was an extension of the working relationship that Dennis Hopper and Peter Fonda had established while making *The Trip*. Roger Corman had allowed Hopper to direct second-unit footage of Fonda in the desert near Palm Springs. Hopper and Fonda had so enjoyed working together that they and a friend, William Heyward, began searching for a movie project they could develop with Roger Corman through AIP. Toward this end, Hopper invited John Gilmore to lunch one afternoon at a restaurant on La Cienega. Hopper and Fonda already had one of Gilmore's screenplays, a surfing story titled *Breaking Hard*, which they had wanted to do but for which they couldn't get financial backing, and Hopper wanted to know what else Gilmore was working on that they might develop.

Gilmore had written a script called *Out-Takes* for another producer, but the promised backing for it hadn't materialized. "It was about two guys who make a big score selling cocaine," Gilmore said, "and who take off cross-country on their motorcycles looking for their version of paradise, only to get blown away at the end by a guy with a shotgun. I told the plot to Dennis at lunch. He seemed very interested in the story, but he and Peter were having some kind of problem making a deal with AIP, so I didn't hear from him again for a while. It was only after I finally tried to get my surfer script back from Brooke [Hopper's then-wife, Brooke Hayward] that Dennis called me to say he wouldn't use my biker script and that they were going to develop an idea that Peter had suggested."

The idea was *Easy Rider*, which they were developing under the working title *Riding Easy*, allegedly a play on Gilmore's surfer-story title, *Breaking Hard*, and which was about two guys who make a lot of money selling cocaine and who ride their steel steeds east in search of America, finding it personified by a shotgun-wielding redneck. Gilmore said that the rest of the film bore no resemblance to the story he had outlined for Hopper at their luncheon meeting. "I didn't have the part Jack played [the Southern lawyer] or anything like that," he said. "It was just the basic idea. All I would have gotten for it was a few hundred dollars and story credit, but I'd have been satisfied with that."

To lend the project credibility as something other than just another low-budget Peter Fonda motorcycle film, Hopper and Fonda employed novelist Terry Southern to work with them in fashioning a twelve-page treatment or synopsis of the story, which Fonda took to Corman and to AIP and which all found interesting. What AIP didn't find interesting was that Hopper intended to direct the picture. AIP's president, Sam Arkoff, had no reason to trust Hopper with such a project; Hopper was an intelligent and talented actor who had once been a major-studio contract player, but he had never directed a film, and in those days he had a reputation for being wildly unstable. As Jack said of him in 1970, after the making of *Easy Rider*, "I don't think they [Hopper and Fonda] would've gotten the money just for a picture directed by Dennis Hopper. I mean, if you know Dennis, you just don't turn over some money to him and say 'no problem,' you know what I mean?"[2] Arkoff wanted a director he could trust to bring the picture in on time and on budget, but Hopper and Fonda were adamant. Still, they didn't want to walk away from a deal with AIP, so they presumably left it unsettled while they quietly shopped around for another backer.

Jack and Bob Rafelson were just beginning principal photography on *Head* when Hopper and Fonda stopped by the Columbia lot to see them. They brought in another film project for Raybert's consideration, but mentioned the biker project and AIP's interest and the fact that they might have to settle for AIP's terms. They had the treatment of *Easy Rider* with them. Jack and Rafelson read it and, while Hopper and Fonda waited in the office, they took it immediately to Bert Schneider. Schneider suggested that the boys hold off settling with AIP until they heard from him; he thought he could work out a deal with Columbia Pictures to help finance and distribute the film. Schneider took the project to Columbia's New York City headquarters. According to director Richard Rush, Schneider also screened several of Rush's films there—including *Psych-Out* and *Hell's Angels on Wheels*—to show Columbia executives the techniques he intended to employ in the making of *Easy Rider*; indeed, Schneider would use much the same film crew as Rush had used, including cinematographer Laszlo Kovacs, whom many considered a master at handling the then-unstable hand-held camera. One can imagine the film Schneider proposed to Columbia from remarks made by Richard Rush years after *Easy Rider* was released; he pointed out that the production values of *Easy Rider* were much like those of his own films, which he alleged had been screened not only for the Columbia executives but also for the cast

65

and crew before *Easy Rider* was filmed. "They [*Easy Rider* and Rush's films] . . . had in common a lot of storytelling style of proceeding episodically through the piece, where the impact of whatever you're saying emerges through the results of the episodes—that business of playing against the material, like using motorcycles and cutting the sound effects, and handling them lyrically with the right kind of rock music accompaniment, rather than scored music; and, of course, a lot of techniques that Laszlo [Kovacs] and the crew had developed, with me through our past pictures."[3] Such techniques appealed to the under-thirty age group, and Columbia was eager to capitalize on that appeal.

By the time filming had begun on *Easy Rider*, Jack was wrapping up his postproduction work on *Head* and was presumably in the preproduction phase of a picture he would eventually direct called *Drive, He Said*. But Schneider persuaded him to join the *Easy Rider* crew. He was ostensibly sent on location as a technical advisor, but in fact Schneider wanted him there as a trouble-shooter to get the production back on track—and to appear in the film.

Hollywood insiders who were not connected with the film found tales of the shoot greatly amusing. It was believed that Hopper and Fonda were behaving as irresponsible children who had been turned loose to play with motorcycles and cameras and a seemingly inexhaustible supply of film and who were "shooting everything and anything that popped into their heads a with a total self-indulgence that approached the point of thumb-sucking."[4] The shoot had seemed a paragon of indirection from its onset, and had apparently degenerated into something resembling an Alice-in-Wonderland pot party, with Dennis Hopper acting the Mad Hatter's part.

Into this bizarre scenario stepped Rip Torn, a fine actor who had been signed to play the part of George Hanson, a straight-laced but disillusioned Southern lawyer turned alcoholic who gets the Hopper and Fonda characters out of jail and then joins them on the road. Torn has never elaborated publicly about his brief and volatile involvement with the production, but it's said that he wasn't happy with the chaotic atmosphere of the location shoot and unhappier still that the part he had been signed to play was not only poorly delineated, but also hastily and badly written. He asked for rewrites but Hopper refused to accommodate him. They argued bitterly. "I said, 'Screw you,' " Hopper said later, "and that's basically what came down there."[5] Torn quit the production, allegedly judging it "excremental." So already a good actor had quit the film in disgust, and meanwhile Hopper was shipping back a great deal of footage that almost everyone found baffling and that some thought unsalvageable.

Bert Schneider presumably thought that Jack could exert a restraining influence on location. He also wanted Jack to play the part that Rip Torn had vacated. During story conferences for Head, Jack often acted out the parts and had so fascinated Schneider and Rafelson that they planned to use him in future productions as an actor, even though he wanted to concentrate on directing. Hopper bridled at the idea of using Jack in the film. He was determined to cast someone with a legitimate Texas accent. And he considered Jack wrong for the part. "I'd never seen Jack do anything like that," he said. "I saw him as a Hollywood flasher, not as a country bumpkin."[6] Schneider insisted, pointing out to Hopper that he had taken an enormous chance in letting Hopper direct and that he had never asked for anything in return. Feeling indebted to Schneider, Hopper reluctantly agreed to let Jack play the part of George Hanson, and Jack—just as reluctantly—agreed to play it.

Director Henry Jaglom was with Jack when he prepared to leave for the Easy Rider location shoot. Jaglom had first worked with Jack as an actor when Jack got him a part as his sidekick in Psych-Out. "I went downstairs with him at the old Columbia [studio] to the barbershop when he got his hair cut for Easy Rider," Jaglom said, "and he was very annoyed at that, because he didn't want to do the part. He had a lot of other things going, and they had just gotten through this complicated and devastating thing with Head. But he went down there and got his hair cut, and reluctantly went off to Texas, or wherever it was, to do Easy Rider."[7]

Sending someone like Jack to coax the boys into responsible behavior might not have seemed the wisest move Bert Schneider could have made, but he probably had no alternative. As a contemporary of Hopper and Fonda, Jack would not likely alienate them, and any control he could exert would be better than none. As it turned out, he indeed may have brought stability to the production, but he also joined in the craziness and undoubtedly instigated some of it himself. On location in Taos, New Mexico, for example, he and Hopper took LSD and were chauffeured to

67

novelist D. H. Lawrence's tomb in the mountains nearby. Under the drug's influence, they stayed several hours at the tomb. "When we got up there," Jack said, "we were starting to come on. The sun was going down so that it was only slightly above eye level. Dennis and I get very sentimental about each other at these moments; we love to cry about old times and talk about how it's gonna be. So we were up there rapping about D. H. Lawrence and how beautiful it was. We decided we were gonna sit on the tomb with D. H. Lawrence and that was it. From then on, this was where we were going to make our stand in life, and if they wanted to go on with the movie, they'd have to come up here and get us; 'cause this was where we were and this was where we'd be."[8]

Someone in the production unit did go to the tomb and get them that evening, and back in town—still very much under the influence but apparently aware that he was in the Wild West—Jack stood guard for a while over their motel rooms, fully expecting an Indian attack. Eventually, he forgot about Indians and wandered off alone. He climbed to the top of a forty-foot tree to watch the sunrise. When light broke, he discovered that the strangely shaped "rocks" he had been admiring from his perch were actually cattle on an open range. He climbed from the tree and followed the herd around the meadow for a while and came upon a dog's plastic squeaker toy shaped like a pork chop, which he took back to his motel and which he carried in his pocket through most of the filming.

Fortunately, the Columbia executives and producer Bert Schneider were blissfully unaware that the representative Schneider had sent on location to protect their half-million-dollar investment had instead been protecting a New Mexico motel against a possible Indian attack, hallucinating in a tree, and secretly carrying a plastic pork chop in his pocket.

A decision had been made to include a marijuana scene in the film, and rather than simply act stoned—as the participants would have acted drunk from liquor, had the script called for it, the campfire scene was shot with Jack and Dennis Hopper totally under the drug's influence. Years later, Jack described their difficulty in handling the scene. "Each time I did a take or angle," Jack said, "it involved smoking almost an entire joint. We were smoking regular dope, pretty good Mexican grass for the state of Michoacán.

Now, the main portion of this sequence is the transition from not being stoned to being stoned. So that after the first take or two, the acting job becomes reversed. Instead of being straight and having to act stoned at the end, I'm now stoned at the beginning and have to act straight and then gradually let myself return to where I was—which was very stoned. It was an unusual reverse acting problem. And Dennis was hysterical offcamera most of the time this was happening; in fact, some of the things that you see in the film—like my looking away and trying to keep myself from breaking up—were caused by my looking at Dennis offcamera over in the bushes, totally freaked out of his bird, laughing his head off while I'm in there trying to do my Lyndon Johnson and keep everything together."[9] (Jack modeled the Texas accent he used in the film after that of then–President Lyndon Johnson. He also drew upon his grandfather, John Nicholson, for his portrayal of George Hanson—alcoholic, quiet, melancholic, a soft man—and wore glasses exactly like those his grandfather wore.)

After the film was wrapped—or, as one observer wryly put it, after the boys finally had to quit shooting because they had used up all their film—they went back to Hollywood and screened the footage to find the motion picture they had shot. It was a sobering experience. Merely viewing the hours and hours and hours of film was confusing and mind-numbing and depressing and exhausting. They finally cut the footage into sections and, under Schneider's supervision, nearly everyone did some cutting on it. Hopper worked on the road scenes; Fonda worked on the psychedelic graveyard scene; Jack worked on his own scenes, adding, for example, the scene where he is wearing a gold football helmet and riding on the back of Peter Fonda's motorcycle, and smiling and waving directly at the camera. Jack was waving at the camera crew, and the footage was never intended for inclusion in the film, but he added it, thereby establishing direct eye contact and rapport with the audience, an old device often employed by the likes of Laurel and Hardy and one that worked as effectively for Jack, resulting in one of the film's most engaging moments.

The "platoon" editing plan failed to reduce the footage to manageable proportions or to reveal avenues of continuity that might be pursued. John Gilmore saw a screening of this "edited" footage and was appalled. "The film was about ten hours long," Gilmore

69

said, "and it was just nonsense. No one could believe how bad that footage was."

What finally emerged from the cutting room was a minor miracle. The finished film was flawed, and very few scenes play well today, but it took a truly inspired editor to have done anything at all with the material. If any film can be said to have been made in the cutting room, it was *Easy Rider*.

People in the motion picture industry didn't pay much attention to the film when it was released; they considered it just another motorcycle picture until its box-office grosses indicated that it had struck a responsive chord with a large audience. And while the moviegoer couldn't have cared less how the picture had been put together, moviemakers and film buffs and critics were still wondering years later who had edited the final version that eventually brought in about $40 million; they had heard that before the final cut the footage had resembled nothing more than the outtakes of dozens of films spliced together. Those who worked on the film were friends and were more than a little reluctant to discuss the subject frankly or to claim credit that might detract from Hopper's directorial accomplishment.

Screen credit for the editing was given to Donn Cambern, for he did the finished cutting and splicing once it was decided what should be cut. The final editing was done by Henry Jaglom. When everyone had finished working with his own section of footage, Schneider hired Jaglom to bring a semblance of order, if not continuity, to the film. Jaglom spent ten weeks doing so. His work was subject to Schneider's approval, of course, and he also considered the feelings and wishes of his buddies Jack, Dennis Hopper, and Peter Fonda whenever possible—often leaving scenes in that might better have been shortened or cut completely—but there is no doubt that it was Jaglom who shaped the footage into what came to be known as *Easy Rider*.

Though Jaglom can't deny that he spent two and a half months of his life in a dark cutting room organizing the mismatched pieces of a filmic jigsaw puzzle, he insists that his task was simply that of pulling together what Dennis Hopper had, in Jaglom's words, "brilliantly" directed and had been trying to convey. Jaglom said the same of Bert Schneider's work, whose role in the project he likened to that of a writer's editor, curbing Hopper's excesses and helping

70

to focus his material. While true in part, a more appropriate application of the analogy would have been to liken Hopper to a writer who tosses his editor a dictionary he has written, asking him to pull some words from it to form a novel he has in mind—an exaggeration, but no more so than calling Hopper's effort "brilliant."

It was evident even from the earliest box-office receipts that *Easy Rider* was going to be one of the year's most successful films. There had been a generation or two of young Americans who had been brought up with the Bomb, a seemingly endless undeclared war in Vietnam, and the assassination of its political and civil rights leaders who saw the film as an expression of the alienation and disillusionment they felt at what they considered the perversion of the American Dream by the Establishment. For them, *Easy Rider* symbolized the Cold War between the straight society, which they perceived as anesthetized, and their own, and growing, countercultural society. Jack's role as George Hanson, the disillusioned alcoholic attorney son of a wealthy and prominent Texas family, is a pivotal one. Not only does he escape conformity—which in itself makes him the hero of the piece—but he's also the only multidimensional character in the film, and therefore the only one with whom the audience can empathize. His death is tragic, while the death of the two dope-dealing bikers, though as senseless, is merely shocking and sad.

The whole of *Easy Rider* is larger than the sum of its parts, and its appeal in its day as something commonly felt but never before expressed in a mass medium is not apparent when viewed today. There are a few excellent scenes, but the dialogue and minitours of countercultural lifestyles and endless shots of the countryside often seem inept and pointless. It was not timeless art, but propaganda: a film of and for its brief moment. In this, it was enormously effective.

As the film took shape, it was evident to many that despite the brevity of Jack's cameo appearance, he was making the film his own, eclipsing the film's stars. Jane Fonda was making *They Shoot Horses, Don't They?* with Bruce Dern at the time, and according to Dern, she raved daily about Jack Nicholson's performance. Like almost everyone else, Dern was skeptical. He had appeared in and seen enough low-budget motorcycle pictures to last a lifetime. And as for the notorious pot-smoking scene, it seemed to Dern inevitable that someone would eventually get around to shooting one—just another gimmick. "I didn't think much of it [the film]," he said, "and then *Easy Rider* comes out and goes blam!"[10]

Before its general release, the film was entered in the Cannes Film Festival, and Jack was there. The audience was respectful and attentive, but when his first scene came on, there was an electrified murmur that rippled in waves throughout the audience. "I'm one of the few people who was actually present at the moment I became a star," he said of the experience. "I mean, I could actually sense it in the audience. . . . It was great."[11]

Easy Rider was named Best First Film at the festival, but Jack's performance wasn't honored, because supporting players aren't given awards at Cannes. Back home, though, he was named Best Supporting Actor by the New York Film Critics and was nominated for an Oscar by the Academy of Motion Picture Arts and Sciences. Jack lost the Oscar to Gig Young for Young's supporting role in *They Shoot Horses, Don't They?*

Even so, Jack's performance and the critical attention it generated as well as his nomination for an Academy Award were enough to establish him as a rising star. And Jack Nicholson was ready. "I was thirty-two years old," he said later, "and I'd been working at it a long time and watched a lot of people go through the process. I watched mistakes, I watched what they did right; I watched why they did what they did—it was all they talked about. And so when the situation of being a movie star presented itself, I knew like nobody ever had what was going on. I knew how to act in movies and select projects and program my career and keep the quality up and make it worth the people's while to see it."[12]

72

> "He's [Jack] easily seduced by anything . . . that suggests the possibility of something splendid or grand."
>
> *Diana Vreeland*[1]

Jack no longer had to take every acting job he was offered just to keep bread on the table and his foot in the industry door. By January 1970, major producers were knocking on *his* door, and he could choose from among them. He was so unused to the experience that at first he committed to more projects than he could comfortably manage—including a musical that was lucrative but a waste of his time.

His private life had also improved. Shortly after his 1968 divorce from Sandra, Jack waded into a sea of women; for a while, he was, in his words, a "walking cliché" of the predatory male. But he wasn't happy. Despite his apparently insatiable need to chase women who are not in his grasp, he was beginning to sense what he later would discover in therapy: that whatever pleasure he finds in his private life is almost wholly dependent

8

CHANGES

upon his satisfying an even more urgent need for the support of a special woman in his life. Perhaps as a rebellion against the knowledge of this monogamous dependency, he has often played the role of Playboy of the Western World. He cultivated this image early in his career—one that the show-business media exaggerated but that gave him a slight tarnish he thought might be "good for business." In fact, though he's still apparently dazzled by and on occasion chases after what he and his friend Warren Beatty call "skunks"— that is, attractive and seemingly unattainable or unapproachable women, who are especially personified for Jack by high-fashion models—the satisfaction he gets from skirt-chasing is transitory and unfulfilling. For this reason, he nurtures long-term relationships, which he never consciously severs and which usually end only when his companion realizes that Jack's idea of a relationship is what might be called "flexible monogamy": You be monogamous and and flexible, and I'll be me. So after the skirt-chasing binge that followed his divorce, he settled into the first such relationship, this one with Mimi Machu, and it lasted several years.

Mimi was beautiful and smart. She also had other qualities necessary to live with the likes of Jack Nicholson: a good sense of humor, inordinate patience, and a fiery nature that kept him off balance and interested. She didn't adopt his philosophy of "flexible monogamy," though, and so like all of Jack's serious relationships, theirs was a stormy one. "We were two maniacs who couldn't live together or apart," Mimi said of their years together.[2] For a while, though, their relationship was new and exciting to Jack, and he was busy with his suddenly burgeoning career, too preoccupied for chasing "skunks." Their first years together were relatively harmonious.

Even though Jack had Mimi with whom to share his excitement at becoming a star, success would have been more gratifying to him had June lived to see him become famous. June and Ethel May were the people to whom he had most wanted to prove himself, the two whose opinion he valued and whose esteem he undoubtedly coveted, and they had resigned themselves to his "failure." June had died six years earlier, of course, and that left Ethel May, who would have taken pride in Jack's stardom and who would have benefited greatly from it. However, this, too, was not meant to be.

On the evening of January 6, 1970, Ethel May died.[3] She was

74

seventy-one and had been chronically ill for a long time. In the early 1960s, she had moved to California so that June could care for her. She had been there only a short time when June got cancer and died. Jack and Sandra were expecting Jennifer at the time, and were in no position to care for Ethel May, so she had returned to New Jersey to be back among her friends and to live with Lorraine and Shorty.

Jack went back to New Jersey for Ethel May's funeral. He had not yet learned the truth of his birth, and he still believed Ethel May was his natural mother. He asked to be left alone with her in the viewing room at the funeral home and sat for more than an hour beside her casket, examining his feelings for her and feeling, as he said, the grief and the loss. It had been sixteen years since he had left home. Nothing is known of his relationship with Ethel May during those years; Jack has always been guarded and evasive on this subject. He has said only that he had had an "understanding" with his family, intimating that he had taken charge of his own life at a very early age and had expected from them a minimum of interference in his personal affairs.

During the hour or so that he spent with Ethel May in the viewing room, he came to the conclusion that he had communicated his love for her over the years and that he had fulfilled whatever expectations of him she had had. "I didn't feel any sense of 'Oh, I wish I had done this or that,' at the moment of bereavement," he said.[4] Ethel May was buried on January 10, 1970.

In the few interviews he gives, Jack still pays tribute to Ethel May, citing her as one of his models of self-reliance and lamenting that she supported everyone until she was no longer able to walk or work and that she died a charity case, implying, perhaps, that she hadn't lived long enough for him to pay her back for all she had done. Though he has never said as much, he probably takes solace in the fact that Ethel, unlike June, did live to see him on the threshold of success; he had been nominated for an Academy Award, had finished filming a cameo in a Paramount musical, was set to star in another film to be released by Columbia, and was preparing to make his debut as a director with a film of his own. Whether or not she had been well enough to be aware of his accomplishments isn't known.

The musical Jack did with Paramount—his first film after *Easy*

Rider—was *On a Clear Day You Can See Forever,* and his signing to do it seemed to negate his contention that he knew exactly what to do once he had become a star. The picture wasn't very good and neither was the role he signed to play. To others, it seemed an awkward career move. Interviewers still ask why he did the film. Bored with the question, he usually dismisses it by saying he did it for the money. Though money wasn't the only factor, it was an important one this time. He wanted to buy a house—a place of his own—and he presumably needed the money Paramount was offering him in order to do so. He bought a house on Mulholland Drive in the low Santa Monica Mountain range that separates Beverly Hills from the San Fernando Valley, and he has lived there ever since.

The place on Mulholland Drive is a relatively modest two-story house with eight rooms. It faces north, with a view of the San Fernando Valley below. The back overlooks the canyons, and there's a wooden deck with a swimming pool off an enclosed patio that borders the living and dining rooms. Jack later had a balcony built off his upstairs master bedroom, with a gate built into the guardrail so that he can jump from the balcony into the swimming pool. He also had an open-air hot tub carved into the bedrock; it can be reached from a downstairs bathroom. There is a living room with a fireplace, a den with a wall-size television set, an upstairs office lined with bookshelves, and other bedrooms—one of them a servant's room off the kitchen, which is often used by houseguests.

In time, the house was filled with art works, including sculptures and fine prints. Jack is interested mostly in paintings, however; they now line the walls of the rooms and hallways, upstairs and down, including the bathrooms. When he ran out of wall space, he began stacking them in the guest bedroom. An art magazine recently named him one of the sixty top private art collectors in the United States. Ethel May had been a fairly good amateur artist and had often done portraits of Jack when he was a boy. He presumably became interested in art through her. He has some of her work, and it hangs with the likes of Picasso, Magritte, Matisse, and de Lempica.

Jack later bought the house next door, enlarging his compound, but the feature of the location that he found most intriguing—and that may have been his primary reason for buying that particular place at a time when he couldn't afford it—was the third house that shared his private drive off Mulholland. It's owned by one of his acting idols, Marlon Brando, and it sits on the hill just above Jack's. Jack was moving closer to Brando in more ways than one, and he was not the kind to overlook the metaphorical aspect of his move.

There were other reasons for doing the Paramount musical apart from earning the money to buy the house. For one, Jack worried about being typecast, and a Hollywood musical was a wide departure from his *Easy Rider* role. Years later, he said of his taking such divergent parts, "If I hadn't broken from it [the stereotypical mold] right at the beginning, they wouldn't let me play anything but *Easy Rider*."[5] Another factor was that he was flattered that directors such as Vincente Minnelli and Mike Nichols wanted to work with him. He wanted to see what it would be like to work in a Vincente Minnelli musical. As his friend former *Vogue* editor Diana Vreeland once said of Jack, "He's easily seduced by anything—object, man, woman—that suggests the possibility of something splendid or grand." Jack was particularly vulnerable to such grand offers at this early stage of his stardom, and a Hollywood musical starring Barbra Streisand and directed by Vincente Minnelli, who had done fine musicals like *An American in Paris* and *The Band Wagon*, was just too glamorous an offer for him to resist.

Jack had no way of knowing how inconsequential his role in the film would be. His character wasn't even in the script when he was approached to do it. Someone involved with the production apparently decided that his phenomenal appeal in *Easy Rider* with young moviegoers could be cashed in on at the box office, and so he was hurriedly added to the picture even before his part was; when he signed to do it, Jack knew only that he'd get a chance to sing in the film and that his voice wouldn't be dubbed by someone else. He had always loved music, and the prospect intrigued him.

Director Vincente Minnelli auditioned Jack and signed him—according to Jack—because of his singing voice. "I auditioned," Jack said, "just me and him in the room, a cappella—me singing 'Don't Blame Me' to Vincente Minnelli—it blew my mind!"[6]

Jack played the part of Tad Pringle, Barbra Streisand's stepbrother, who was supposed to be a well-to-do hippie. But apparently no one connected with the production had the faintest idea what a hippie was, and the first thing they asked of Jack was for him to get a haircut for the role. Then wardrobe outfitted him in sweaters, slacks, and sport coats, and gave him a sitar to strum during his duet with Streisand—all of which made him look more like a polyester beatnik than a hippie.

His biggest disappointment with the project was with Minnelli. Ever the aspiring director, and always wanting to work with and learn from the best, Jack had anticipated watching Minnelli in action. The director didn't work with him much, though. "You have to sort of guess what he wants," Jack said of him later. "One day I said, 'Look, Vincente, I really don't mind being directed.' "[7] Since his role in the picture was parenthetical, there wasn't much that he or a director could do with it.

Jack had misgivings after he finished the shooting. "I'm very frightened about it, I'll be perfectly honest," he told columnist Rex Reed shortly before the film's release. "I don't know how I come off. . . . If I can bear that moment when I'll finally have to sit there with my friends and watch myself sing . . . then I think it will be worth it."[8]

He needn't have worried. All that remained of his role in the film's final version was a brief and pointless scene. His duet with Streisand had been cut. The film and his participation in it were largely ignored by critics and moviegoers. A *Time* critic did note Jack's "minuscule" role and called his performance a "giant step backwards from *Easy Rider*." Ultimately, it proved to be just an inconsequential side step, and it was forgotten after his next picture.

78   With the success of their film *Easy Rider*, producers Bert Schneider and Bob Rafelson expanded production and took on another partner, Steve Blauner, changing their company name from Raybert to BBS Productions (an acronym for Bert, Bob, and Steve) and maintaining their affiliation with Columbia Pictures for financing and distribution. One of their first projects was *Five Easy Pieces*. Bob Rafelson had been working on elements of the film's story line for a while, but when Jack walked away with *Easy Rider* and an Academy Award nomination, Rafelson got together with Carol Eastman to fashion the story line as a starring vehicle for Nicholson. Rafelson directed the film; it was shot by *Easy Rider* cinematographer Laszlo Kovacs; and it featured Karen Black, Susan Anspach, and a bit player, Sally Struthers, in her first film.

Carol Eastman wrote the screenplay, allegedly modeling the film's protagonist, Bobby Dupea, as a composite of both her brother and Jack. It's usually pointless and foolish to compare an actor's own personality to that of the character he's portraying, but in this instance it's interesting to note that Jack has mentioned similarities between himself and Bobby Dupea and has emphasized that the part was written expressly for him by someone who knew him, in his words, "very, very well" and who even added incidents to the script from his own experiences—such as the restaurant scene described in Chapter 3.

The character Bobby Dupea is a concert pianist turned drifter who has drifted from his refined family of classical musicians, from lasting relationships, and from responsibility; he's a talented and intelligent man driven to live only for the moment and at odds with himself for doing so. "I move around a lot," he tells his ailing father, "not because I'm looking for anything, but because I'm getting away from things that get bad if I stay."

As the film opens, Dupea is working as an oil-field rigger on the California edge of the Mojave Desert and is living with a simple, backwoodsy woman named Rayette (Karen Black). It's evident that bad stuff has been bunching up on him faster than he can drift: his drifter pal is arrested; he discovers Rayette is pregnant; he quits his job; and he learns that his father is gravely ill and paralyzed as a result of two strokes, and that he's expected home to see him. The scene where Bobby tries to explain to his father why he bolted the family and a promising career for the life of a beer-swilling, skirt-chasing carouser was a poignant one for Jack, one in which he drew upon elements of his own life and which resulted in an acting breakthrough for him. It was a scene that caused a friendly but heated confrontation between Jack and director Bob Rafelson during the shooting.

Rafelson considered the scene pivotal and thematically essential to the delineation of Bobby Dupea's character. He feared that Jack would understate the emotion, play the part too coolly, too unsympathetically. It is a scene in which Bobby attempts to explain to his father why he is wasting his talent, frittering away his life, why he has failed to meet his family's expectations of him. Rafelson felt that Bobby would be contrite at the meeting with his father. "So we were down to a few scenes," Jack said later of the confrontation with Rafelson, "and he was nakedly now saying to me, 'Hey, I want you to cry in this movie.' Now that's one thing, as an actor, you never say. You don't go for an emotion—or one doesn't if they work the way I do. And this is the last kind of direction you want to hear. But everything is not class. This is the professional game."[9]

Jack fought against Rafelson's interpretation, contending that contrition was inappropriate, that it would seem pitiful and that a man such as Dupea would never entertain self-pity. They argued half the night and through part of the following morning. Rafelson was adamant. Finally, he said, "Jack, this is bullshit. You don't want to do it because you can't!"[10]

Jack eventually gave in. Long before their disagreement, he had crossed out the scene in his copy of the script and had written "something else?" in the margin. But now that he agreed that the scene would evolve essentially as written, he rewrote the dialogue, thinking of his own "father" (John Nicholson) as he did so and playing the scene as though it were John Nicholson sitting in the wheelchair before him. They shot the scene that morning, and it was one of the film's best; it couldn't have been played better, and Jack was proud of it. "On take one, away I went," he said, "and I think it was a breakthrough. It was a breakthrough for me as an actor, for actors. I don't think they'd had this level of emotion, really, in almost any male character until that point. You know, an actor hears the difference when an actor touches that level of emotion for real."[11]

It was such a memorable experience for him that fifteen years and many films later he still had strong sensory impressions of that day's shooting. He remembered the grass on the hill, and what the air was like, and what happened after the scene was shot. Even so, it was a long time before Jack appreciated the performance that Bob Rafelson had pulled out of him against his will; for a few years afterward, he grumbled that Bobby Dupea wouldn't have lost his composure like that. He recently revealed that he had played the role as an allegory of his own career, which accounts for the personal offense he took at playing the scene Rafelson's way; in effect, he was saying that Jack Nicholson would not have lost control as Bobby did. Under similar circumstances, Jack would have agonized privately, might have lain on his shoes in the closet afterward, but he wouldn't have revealed himself as Rafelson made Bobby Dupea do, not even to his father. This is precisely why even people who are fairly close to Jack find him inscrutable, why such friends as actress Candice Bergen say that he's "basically unknowable." Even the private Jack Nicholson persona is, in essence, a role he's playing.

During the filming of *Five Easy Pieces*, Sally Struthers developed a schoolgirl crush on Jack, once even knocking on his door in the middle of the night to get his attention. Jack didn't let her in; he treated her as a kid sister and sent her back to her quarters. Probably one of his reasons for not responding to her advances was that he was already having an affair at the time with another woman in the cast—Susan Anspach. In the film, Anspach portrayed a woman who is attracted to Bobby and who has a one-day affair with him, only to break it off when she realizes that he's incapable of committing wholly to anyone or anything. Jack and Susan's offcamera affair was nearly as brief; it ended when the picture wrapped. Nine months later, Susan gave birth to a baby boy, whom she named Caleb. Jack says he knew nothing of the birth and that he didn't learn until years later that Susan was telling close friends that he was the boy's father. In 1980, there was a published report claiming that Jack had finally admitted publicly what he had always maintained privately: that Caleb was his son.[12]

Writer Nancy Collins interviewed Jack in 1984 and asked him about Susan Anspach's claim. Jack demurred. "She says that all the time," he told Collins, "but because of the way she's been toward me, I've never been allowed a real avenue to find out about it. That's her privacy. She's an avant-garde feminist who—when I met her—was proud of the fact that she already had a child whose father no one knew. She didn't mention her second child to me until six or seven years later." Jack said he had tried to telephone Susan about the boy "a couple of times," but had not reached her, and that he wasn't convinced that he's the boy's father. "But I haven't had the opportunity to look into it," he said. "I know Susan slightly and feel she's an extremely respectable person who is powerful, smart and, I'm sure, in very good control of what she does. And I guess I like the idea in a certain way . . . if it were true. Hey, I'm ready to meet anybody. Do you know what I mean? And that's all I can say about it."[13]

Helena Kallianiotes also had a small and humorous part in the picture as one of two women hitchhikers. Kallianiotes is an actress whom Jack befriended and took in during a low point in her life and career and who has stayed on ever since in the house next to his, cooking for him and managing his household, while continuing to act.

Jack was nominated for an Academy Award as Best Actor for his part in *Five Easy Pieces* and was delighted to be recognized by the Academy for his first starring role since his discovery. He was in the audience at the awards ceremony, and thoroughly enjoyed himself. In the days when he was outside looking in, he used to say of the ceremonies, "Who wants to sit under sixty-seven flood-lights for four hours without even being able to go out to take a leak?" But that was the old days. Now, he says, "Unstylistically, I love the Academy Awards. And I'm very Fifties Zen—all tributes are false, all is vanity—but I like seeing a Mount Rushmore of . . . movie stars in a row for the night, no matter what nutty ideas they've got. It's fun. Nobody gets hurt. With a couple of exceptions, I've known whether I was going to win or not because I've been following these things since I was a kid. And I've always had a better time when I know I'm not going to win, because then I'm just into the evening. I'm Mr. Hollywood."[14] On this occasion, he had looked over the competition and decided that George C. Scott should and would win for his role in *Patton,* and Scott did. But in effect, Jack won more than an Oscar. He was firmly established in the Mount Rushmore of movie stars himself that night, for the financial success of *Five Easy Pieces* and his nomination as Best Actor proved what had needed to to be proved: that he could carry a picture in a leading role.

Jack was delighted to have proved himself as an actor and to be sought after by big-name producers and directors. That was no longer enough, though. Acting was a performing or interpretive art, one that he enjoyed and that he wanted to continue, but it offered little outlet for the creative drive awakened in him after he had sampled a few of moviemaking's creative arts—writing, editing, and directing—while working with Monte Hellman and with the Corman stock company. Despite the fame and fortune within his grasp as an actor, he was determined—indeed, driven—to take the path he had begun forging before he did *Easy Rider*. For that, he went back to BBS and to the work he had begun two years earlier.

The project was *Drive, He Said*, a film adaptation of a novel by Jeremy Larner that Jack would direct but would not appear in. His interest in

9
NEW
DIRECTIONS

adapting the novel to the screen dated back to 1967 when Fred Roos—the producer who had worked with Jack and Monte Hellman on *Back Door to Hell* and *Flight to Fury*—optioned Larner's novel and approached Larner and Jack to write the screenplay. Both agreed, but the collaborative effort was never begun because Roos couldn't get financial backing for it. The project languished until BBS gave Jack a chance to direct two years later. He flew back to New York and again got Larner's commitment to cowrite the script with him, but shortly afterward he was sidetracked by *Easy Rider* and by the two films that followed.

The story of *Drive, He Said* takes place on an Ohio college campus during the Vietnam War and concerns a college basketball star and his campus-radical roommate. The novel was written in the early 1960s and was prophetic with respect to the campus unrest that was to come, but by the time financial backing was found to bring it to the screen, several films that exploited the situation on college campuses in the mid-1960s—such as *Getting Straight* and *The Strawberry Statement*—were already released or in production. Jack was confident that Larner's story would be more substantive than the others, but he had reservations about coming out with another film staged against campus unrest; he knew it was a risky commercial venture, but he eventually decided that it was worth the risk because its setting was conducive to exploring elements of the human condition that he thought should be brought to the screen.

He was given a relatively small budget of $800,000 and chose **84** Oregon as the location for the filming. He cast his *Five Easy Pieces* costar, Karen Black, and William Tepper in the leads, and among the supporting players were his friends Robert Towne, Henry Jaglom, and Bruce Dern. Had Jack concentrated solely on directing, the experience might have been less trying and more rewarding—but he didn't. Owing largely to his inexperience, he apparently felt the need to touch and taste every aspect of its production, so he saddled himself not only with directing the film but also with coproducing and cowriting it—and more. Given enough time, these tasks might not have been overwhelming, but in his eagerness to direct and in his lack of experience at pacing himself, he forced his project into a space between two acting commitments that did not allow him room to maneuver.

Owing to his work in *Five Easy Pieces*, he was unable to begin shooting *Drive* before the early spring of 1970, and he was committed to report to the East Coast that June for his role in *Carnal Knowledge*, to be directed by Mike Nichols. To meet his commitments, he had to start shooting *Drive* with an unfinished script. Larner had written the first draft of the screenplay and Jack was supposed to have done the second, but he had run out of time to finish it. Meanwhile, Larner had written a third draft, and Jack finally shot the film from his own unfinished draft, interpolated with elements of Larner's new draft and with scenes written on location by Jack, Larner, and Robert Towne.

Once the shooting was under way, Jack squandered time and energy doing menial tasks that should have been delegated to others. Karen Black noted that he was being "run ragged," with more of a burden than a first-time director should have had, even including mundane tasks like picking up costumes for a day's shooting. Bruce Dern also felt that Jack was disorganized and handicapped in trying to direct within the time constraints and around all the production problems. "He was definitely ready to direct his first picture," Dern said, "but he was not ready to direct it without more help than he had going in."[2]

To complicate matters further, representatives of the Directors Guild came around when Jack was about halfway into the shoot and insisted that he join their organization. Jack didn't want to, and so the Guild shut down production for a short time. "We were shooting in the gymnasium," Karen Black said, "and they turned the lights out and he just sat there and stuck to his viewpoint, and he won."[3]

Jack wrapped *Drive* just in time to report to the East Coast for work on *Carnal Knowledge*, where he spent his weekdays before the camera and his weekends editing *Drive*. *Carnal Knowledge* was written by playwright and counterculture cartoonist Jules Feiffer, and traces the lives of two men from college to middle age, dealing with their sexual inadequacies and their inability to establish mature relationships with the women in their lives. The film features Candice Bergen, singer Art Garfunkel, and Ann-Margret. Mike Nichols had directed for the Broadway stage, and so he put the cast through two weeks of rehearsals before filming. His painstaking attention to detail and his organizational skills were a revelation to Jack. Aside from Bob Rafelson, Jack had had little opportunity to work with and learn from veteran directors, and he lamented that he had not waited until after studying Mike Nichols's technique before he had tried his own hand at directing.

Director Nichols had the pot smokers in the cast swear off marijuana for the film's duration. He presumably wanted their undivided attention, but he also felt that since Jack was portraying a college undergraduate in the early sequences, he could better simulate the youthful energy the role required if he was not under the influence of the drug. Jack began smoking cigars, instead, and developed a taste for Cuban Monte Cristos, which he has smoked ever since.

Carnal Knowledge was not well received. It was a well-made and interesting film, and the acting was very good, but neither the critics nor the moviegoers liked its negativism. It was banned in the state of Georgia as "obscene" (the court later ruled that it was not), and while the banning undoubtedly drew a larger audience —to see what all the fuss was about—it didn't help the film. Many who saw it hated it, and it didn't take long for word of mouth to shut down the box office.

Jack was disappointed. He felt that *Carnal Knowledge's* direction and acting were deserving of more respect and that those who hadn't seen the film had been put off for the wrong reasons—assuming that the film itself was bad when in fact it was only the subject matter that the moviegoers had disliked. Ann-Margret was eventually nominated for an Oscar; but the efforts of Jack and director Mike Nichols, while praised by a few critics and moviegoers, were generally panned. However, what seemed to rankle Jack more than the film role's effect on his professional life—which was confined mostly to his frustration at not getting another Oscar nomination —was its effect on his personal life. Once again, he had portrayed a male chauvinist who uses women, and women were beginning to attribute his characters' leanings to him personally. "I *played* those characters," Jack said, "I didn't editorialize them. They are legitimate representations of male attitudes of our time, attitudes that result in crippling negativism. I didn't try to make those men any more or less palpable to an audience than others I've played. That would be pandering."[4]

The release of *Carnal Knowledge* coincided with the release of Jack's first directorial effort, *Drive, He Said*, and it turned out to be one of the worst periods of his professional career. Prior to its general release, Jack entered *Drive* in the Cannes Film Festival, with disastrous results. Though an audience of his international peers had enthusiastically acknowledged him as an actor in *Easy Rider* two years earlier, they scorned his effort at directing, and some even booed the film. Their reaction made it obvious that *Drive* was in trouble. By the time it opened in New York City on June 13, 1971, word of its poor showing at Cannes had drifted across the Atlantic and most moviegoers ignored it. A few critics liked it, but most did not.

BBS and Columbia were apparently willing to put up more money to promote *Drive*, but Jack called them off. "When they asked," he said, "I told them not to press the release of it. I didn't do what producers normally do. I thought, Okay, I'm not gonna force somebody to spend a lot of extra money they might not get back. So let it go. Forget it."[5]

Over the years, the film has stood up better than any of the other campus films that dealt with the rebellious 1960s. It's ironic that it still plays well for many of the same reasons that it was criticized and ignored by moviegoers in its day. In handling the material, Jack refused to pander to what he calls his "constituency," the disillusioned generation or two he had mesmerized in his romp through *Easy Rider* and who would gather in the theater to cheer the good guys and jeer the bad Establishment types. Jack gave them no good guys to cheer or bad guys to boo, only people caught up in relationships and events and swept in directions not of their choosing. It was not a bad film, but the story line and setting were passé by the time it was released, and there was no one with whom a partisan audience could identify. Because it explored rather than exploited the conditions of the social and political unrest of its day, it's still an interesting film, while its commercially successful counterparts now seem inconsequential and even silly. As *Newsweek* critic Paul Zimmerman said, though flawed, *Drive* had "honesty and energy." Jay Cocks, reviewing for *Time*, stretched to call the film a "bush-league disaster," but he was on more solid footing in saying that the film might have gone unnoticed if not unmade, but for Jack's celebrity. Then he added, ". . . while other fledgling directors would be allowed to fail in comparative privacy, Nicholson's reputation makes his failure agonizingly public."

What is especially noteworthy about the *Time* critique is that when it was written Jack had played only two small parts as a known actor and had starred in only two films, yet he was already saddled with a bigger-than-life reputation that was overshadowing his work, a reputation that he would rather have been without.

Years later and with characteristic understatement, Jack said of the experience, "I had unhealthy creative responses." Publicly, he appeared to take the failure of his directorial debut philosophically, but in fact it undermined his self-confidence as an aspiring director and dealt a devastating blow to his self-esteem as a creative artist. It took him several years to recover from its effect. "*Drive* hurt him," Bruce Dern said. "He gets very depressed very easily, and very down on himself, and down on the world, and the business, and everybody around."[6]

By the time *Carnal* and *Drive* opened in Los Angeles in August of 1971, Jack's relationship with Mimi Machu had ended. It had lasted almost three years, and the difficulty of sharing Jack Nicholson's life had simply exhausted Mimi's patience. She had had enough of his "skunk"-chasing, his possessiveness, his Irish black moods, his anger, and his temper tantrums. So she left him. He was so crushed when she left that he rushed over to friend Harry Dean Stanton's house. "He was almost incoherent," Stanton later recalled. "I've never seen such despair."[7] It was soon thereafter that Jack began seeing a therapist.

When an interviewer asked him years later why he had entered Reichian therapy, Jack said, "It was prompted by the collapse of a long-standing relationship with a female [Mimi]. It ended before I was ready to be out of it. She felt that I wasn't worth her time. She'd had it. It was very sudden, very abrupt. I was unprepared. I couldn't cope with all the emotion that was released as the result of being cashiered."[8]

The reason Jack couldn't cope with the loss—in effect, feeling abandoned—was undoubtedly owing to his childhood experiences. Those experiences probably have bearing on his extreme possessiveness, as well. One characteristic that the women in his life have found annoying is his inordinate attachment to his possessions. He has been known to call long distance from Europe to see whether he lost his pocket comb en route or simply left it at home, where it would be safe. He's forever misplacing or losing things around the house, such as his car keys, and storming around in an incredible frenzy at their loss. And it seems apparent that what women have found intolerable is his tendency to treat *them* as possessions, which is why he can't bear to lose them and why he does.

It was while in a depressed state from losing Mimi that Jack found a kindred spirit in Michelle Phillips. Michelle had been a model before joining the rock group the Mamas and the Papas as a singer and marrying the leader of that group, songwriter John Phillips. By the time she and Jack got together, though, she had divorced Phillips and had remarried. "When I met her originally," Jack said, "it was under very tempestuous circumstances. She had been married to my good friend Dennis Hopper, but the marriage lasted only eight days. I started taking her out because she was depressed."[9] As their relationship deepened, Jack called Hopper to see whether there would be ill feelings at his taking up with Michelle; Hopper assured him that there wouldn't be.

Though Jack wanted Michelle to move in with him, she refused, owing to the fact that she had a five-year-old daughter, named China, by John Phillips and did not want to complicate the child's life or, presumably, risk a custody suit by cohabitating with a man. As a compromise, Jack bought the house next door to his, and Michelle moved into that one, with Jack's friend and cook, Helena Kallianiotes. It was there she remained for the duration of their relationship.

Meanwhile, Jack went directly from *Carnal Knowledge* into another BBS production—*A Safe Place*, a low-budget film written and directed by *Easy Rider* film editor Henry Jaglom. It was Jaglom's first effort as a director, which was undoubtedly a factor in Jack's agreeing to star in his film, but mostly Jack committed himself because his friendship with Jaglom dated back to the 1960s, when they hung out together at Barney's Beanery and both were studying acting at the West Coast Actors Studio. They had subsequently appeared together in *Psych-Out*, and Jack had employed Jaglom as an actor in *Drive*. Jack worked in the picture for scale, or, in Jaglom's words, "for a color television set."

Henry Jaglom is a bright but undisciplined filmmaker; he makes the kind of movies that might rank him among the geniuses in the business if he had a commercial success among them. Like many such gifted people, however, he refuses to cut away from his interior world or to exert the self-discipline necessary to work within the traditional narrative mold needed for commercial success. Consequently, he has yet to establish his credentials with the industry, and so he is regarded as merely self-indulgent—though he does have an "underground" following among film buffs. One has to approach Jaglom's films almost on a purely sensory level. They are intensely personal and offer the viewer little in the way of objective reality. His themes are usually disillusionment and emotional isolation, how, in his words, "nostalgia kills," how the romanticism of the late thirties and forties—as expressed by parents, schools, music, and films—was a lie, preparing the child for a life that doesn't exist. *A Safe Place* is such a film.

Besides Jack, the film starred Tuesday Weld, Orson Welles, and Phillip Proctor. It's the story of a young woman, Tuesday Weld, who's isolated by her inability to let go of the past—as personified by Orson Welles—and her reluctance to accept the inevitability of the present—personified by Jack and Philip Proctor. Jack enjoyed working on the film. He was intrigued by the fact that Orson Welles was in it, even though they had no scenes together and though Welles's footage had been completed by the time Jack could report for the shooting. Jack had been known to pass up a night on the town in Manhattan to see Welles's *Citizen Kane* once again at one of the art houses. He also enjoyed working with Tuesday Weld, whom he had seen around Hollywood often in the early days but whose league had been beyond reach.

90   Jaglom gave Jack a minimum of direction during the filming. He wanted Nicholson to be himself, and gave him only a broad idea of where they were going with the film. It was highly improvisational, and Jaglom feels that Jack's performance is as near to the real Jack Nicholson as has ever been seen on film. Jaglom has always been a great admirer of Jack's work. In his opinion, Jack's stardom is based not simply upon talent, which Jaglom considers enormous, but also upon style, in the tradition of Tracy, Gable, and Bogart. The careers of many stars rise or fall with the success or failure of their films, Jaglom says, but Jack's star keeps rising regardless of the film's fate, because it's not his films but, rather, his image that people are responding to.

Columbia's publicity department didn't know how to promote *A Safe Place* when it was ready for distribution. It was an offbeat offering. In an attempt at finding an audience, they advertised it as a conventional love story, and the film quietly died.

In the annals of Jack's career, *A Safe Place* was just another digit; it brought to three the number of films he had appeared in since *Five Easy Pieces* that had done nothing for him. His career wasn't stalled, though. It was in neutral. Despite his questionable taste in subject matter, his stock in the movie industry remained high; he was still seen as a star with great potential, and by now he was getting half a million dollars per picture. Unlike most stars, Jack didn't ask for his fee in advance; always the congenial collaborator—even on the financial side of the business—he began the practice of working for minimum scale, taking his guaranteed fee from the box-office grosses. If the picture made money, so did he; if it didn't, then he took a relative loss along with the producer. He had seen stars demand enormous sums in advance and then walk away as the production company sank under the weight of staggering overhead costs. He also had seen film projects shelved because the stars that were needed for their success demanded more money than the film was likely to make. Jack knew this was bad for business. By working for very little money and taking his fee only when the film began earning money, he was in effect investing himself in each of his films. In Jack's words, this was the "only way anyone involved with a film should make money." As he became a bigger box-office draw, he demanded a percentage of the profits beyond his fee. In time, this system made him a very wealthy man.

After being involved with three disappointing films, Jack went back to the filmmaking combination that had been lucky for him. He signed again with BBS/Columbia to do a film directed by Bob Rafelson and photographed by Laszlo Kovacs—*The King of Marvin Gardens*, costarring Bruce Dern and Ellen Burstyn. The film was shot in Atlantic City, New Jersey, near Neptune, and Jack presumably got home to see Lorraine and Shorty during the ten-week shoot. For Jack and Dern, working together again was a most pleasant experience. They had always been friendly rivals—or at least Dern had thought of himself in that way, considering only Jack and Brando his competition in those days. Competitive by nature, Jack went along with the rivalry. Neither was serious enough about it for it to affect their friendship, which was close, even though Dern didn't socialize with Jack's crowd. Being married and more a homebody, Dern had always led a more settled life than Jack. He was a long-distance runner, and not much of a socialite, and he never took drugs. Theirs was a professional friendship, based on a long acquaintance and shared professional experiences, but they always kept in touch by phone.

They hadn't worked together as actors since they'd made the low-budget exploitation film *Psych-Out,* and in the meantime, Dern had gotten breaks in major productions such as *They Shoot Horses, Don't They?*—opposite Jane Fonda—and had finally hit with his starring role in the excellent science-fiction film *Silent Running.* It had been only a short time since he had had to settle for parts in pictures such as *The Incredible Two-Headed Transplant.*

Jack's celebrity, too, was so new that people were still confusing his name with those of golfer Jack Nicklaus and director Mike Nichols. Occasionally, people would recognize Dern and not Jack when they were together. Whenever this happened, Jack would say to them (alluding to Dern's previous science-fiction and fantasy roles in television and films), "Sure, give it all to him. What am I? Just a major movie star, and you're looking at a man who talks to refrigerators!"[10]

In *The King of Marvin Gardens,* Jack played the part of David Staebler, an introverted intellectual. He's a would-be writer turned radio monologuist who wastes his talent and stories on the late-night air, the kind of man whom Jack describes as a "watching character," or a "one-roomer." Dern plays his brother, Jason, who wastes his life as a hustler and womanizer involved with small-time gangsters, and who enlists his brother in one of his grandiose schemes. It's a psychological slice-of-life film involving their relationship as brothers. It was well written, well directed, and very well acted by the entire cast. Many involved with the picture thought it would be a huge artistic and financial success. The public was apparently looking for more entertaining or escapist fair, however, and the film was hardly noticed. Jack was disappointed with the reviews. A few critics liked it, but many influential ones panned it for what Jack thought were fatuous reasons. "I usually don't think critics can hurt a movie," he said, "but that one they hurt. That movie needed a more neutral kind of criticism. One critic disliked it because it was, in his words, a 'typical Rafelson-Nicholson picture' because it was a downbeat dirge about the death of the American dream. Can you imagine someone saying that to Goya? Would they say it to Faulkner? Stop writing all those downbeat stories? No, it's puerile. Any critic who would say a thing like that is inadequate to his profession."[11]

Though he had been reluctant to commit to the project, Jack's next film was to be *Three-Cornered Circle*, a remake of *The Postman Always Rings Twice*. Hal Ashby was set to direct, and he wanted to cast Michelle Phillips as Jack's costar. Ashby thought Phillips very talented. He knew she had a large following among rock fans and thought they would be drawn to the box office. He felt, too, that Phillips's real-life relationship with Jack would add a dimension to the film—that they would be very exciting together. The MGM studio executives didn't share his view and didn't like his casting ideas. They presumably didn't want to take a chance with a former rock singer—newly turned actress—costarring in a big-budget production. So they bridled at Ashby's casting; Ashby bridled at their interference; and the project collapsed.

Meanwhile, Jack had signed to do a $2 million comedy drama for Paramount Pictures, *The Last Detail*, based on Darryl Ponicsan's novel and adapted for the screen by Robert Towne, Jack's friend from his acting-school days. Paramount had yet to chose a director for the film, so when the *Postman* deal failed, Jack suggested Hal Ashby, and Paramount signed him.

Jack had been interested in Ponicsan's novel for a long time. He had read proofs of it while making *Five Easy Pieces*, and had wanted to option the screen rights so that he could play the lead, but he didn't have the money to do so, and Paramount got it. It's the story of two Navy shore-patrol officers—played by Jack and Otis Young—who are charged with escorting a naïve young sailor (Randy Quaid) to prison, and they decide to show him a good time before taking him in. Unlike some of the male stars before him who refused to work with anyone taller than they were, Jack had no second thoughts about working between six-foot-two Otis Young and six-foot-four Randy Quaid. In fact, Jack's such a commanding presence as Billy "Bad Ass" Buddusky that no one really notices or cares about the differences in their heights.

Jack's letter of credit in the industry was more than a little shopworn by the time *The Last Detail* was released. He needed a big critical and financial success, and that's what *Detail* was. It is a fine film and one of Jack's favorite roles. His work in it brought him another Oscar nomination as Best Actor, but the award went to Jack Lemmon that year for *Save the Tiger*.

Michelle Phillips had left Jack by the time *The Last Detail* was wrapped. As he had when Mimi left him, Jack suffered a period of dark despondency that worried some of his friends. He adored Michelle and often had asked her to marry him, but she found him too difficult to deal with. They parted friends, and in time Michelle began seeing Warren Beatty. Just as Jack had called his friend Dennis Hopper to ensure that there would be no ill feelings about his relationship with Michelle, so Michelle called Jack to see whether he would harbor ill feelings if she took up with his friend Beatty. Jack gave them his blessing and said he felt genuinely happy for them, for by this time he had fallen in love with someone new, director John Huston's daughter Anjelica.

Like the house at Fountain and Gardner that he
had rented during the lean years, Jack's place
on Mulholland Drive was an open house whenever
he was there. It was often party time, and this
was the staging area for impromptu shopping
sprees and excursions to restaurants and rock clubs
and sporting events. There seemed to be a steady
flow of people passing through the place at times,
friends, or friends of friends, or acquaintances with
out-of-town visitors in tow. It was at such a gathering at his home in the fall of 1973 that Jack first
saw Anjelica Huston. She was visiting the West
Coast from New York City, and had gone to Jack's
party with a friend. Jack saw her across the room,
a twenty-two-year-old woman of obvious grace
and refinement, a definite thoroughbred, dark and
lovely but totally unaffected. "Class," he said of
his first impression of her, "I saw class."

10

ANJELICA

Anjelica was definitely uncommon. She was the younger of two children born to director John Huston and his wife Enrica Soma, a beautiful Balanchine ballerina whom everyone called Ricki. Anjelica was raised in Galway, Ireland, in a Georgian mansion with servants, formal gardens, a guest house, and a stable of fifty thoroughbred horses. The family's houseguests were the likes of the Rothschilds and Jean-Paul Sartre, as well as writers, artists, and show-business luminaries. Anjelica led an enchanted childhood there. Her mother encouraged imagination above all else, and she kept trunks of costumes in the guest house for the children's use. They and their friends put on plays for themselves and occasionally for their parents and guests. Anjelica says that she and her brother Tony often lived for days at a time as people they made up.

With a slightly older brother and a swashbuckling father who set examples to compete with, her life wasn't all silk and frills and playacting; she did the usual kid stuff, too, tree climbing and dare taking and hunting, and she became a fine horseback rider. Hers was a wonderfully idyllic life on the Emerald Isle until her parents' marital problems surfaced. As one of the world's premiere film directors, John Huston spent much of his time on movie locations around the world, and word of many other beautiful women in his life drifted back to Ireland. In time, John and Ricki's relationship collapsed and they divorced. Anjelica moved to London with her mother, where life was not idyllic but different and challenging. She spent holidays in Ireland.

96   Ricki had a big house in London; it, too, became an enchanting salon, with parties attended by a fascinating variety of people: actors, writers, politicians, and socialites. Anjelica had attended lower school in Ireland and then had had tutors; after the move, she went to the lycée, which she hated. She attended Holland Park Comprehensive as a teenager in the mid-1960s, where, according to her childhood friend Joan Juliet Buck, ". . . the rascal side of her came out. She wore eyeliner and miniskirts and smoked cigarettes and did extraordinary things with her hips when she danced."[2]

It was at this time, age sixteen, that she appeared in her first film. As the daughter of a famous movie director and of a ballerina who had encouraged her playacting, it was natural for Anjelica to aspire to an acting career. To encourage her, John Huston starred her in his film *A Walk with Love and Death,* a decision that he later judged a "terrible mistake. She wasn't ready," he said. "I forced her to do it."[3] The film failed, and the critics were not kind. Shy and inordinately sensitive, Anjelica felt responsible for the failure and believed that she had let her father down. It was a crushing experience, one that undermined her confidence and happened at about the same time that she suffered the most devastating of blows: Her mother was killed in an automobile accident in France.

Shortly after her mother's death, Anjelica went from London to New York City as an understudy for the part of Ophelia in an English production of *Hamlet.* But she had lost confidence in her abilities as an actress and she soon turned to modeling, with almost immediate success. Over the next few years, she posed for many of the elite high-fashion photographers, including Guy Bourdin, Helmut Newton, and Bob Richardson; *Vogue* magazine even devoted thirty pages of one issue to her. She lived with Bob Richardson for a while, but she still lacked confidence, and working with some of the world's most exotic models did nothing to build it, despite her success. "I loved the clothes, the champagne, the attention," she said, "Everything but my own looks. Day after day I shared a mirror with the world's most beautiful women and stared at eyes that were bigger than mine, noses that were smaller. I cried and cried because I thought I was ugly."[4]

By the time she attended the party at Jack's in 1973, her relationship with Richardson had ended. She and Jack were attracted to each other immediately, and the attraction changed both their lives. Within days, they were in love, and within months Anjelica had put the East Coast and her modeling career behind her and had moved in with Jack. It was not an easy transition for her. She was accustomed to being an object of interest as a model; that was her professional self—detached, impersonal, a role that required no social interaction. As the new woman in Jack's frenzied household, however, and subject to appraisal as Jack Nicholson's new love interest by the parade of strangers that passed through his house, it was her private self that was being scrutinized, and that part of her was painfully shy. Anjelica has said that until she adjusted to Jack's crowd, she spent much of her time in the bathroom, throwing up from nerves.

Eventually, her presence had a calming effect on Jack and on the household; the frantic tempo slowed enough for her to adjust. She gave up modeling, became, in her words, "a woman of leisure," and lived Jack's life. Jack's friends were impressed with the way he settled down with Anjelica. He even stopped his "skunk"-chasing sprees—for a while.

"Jack has an almost hypnotic gift of being absolutely present. As with Brando, it is almost impossible to take your eyes from him, even when he seems to be doing nothing."

Robert Hatch[1]

Much of a successful film actor's offcamera time is spent in search of worthy and solid projects to work on, a search that ends in frustration more often than not. There are mountains of scripts to read, tentative offers to explore, projects that surface, take up one's time, then sink before they can be acted upon; there are meetings to attend, negotiations, more meetings, and deals that somehow collapse after months or even years of preliminary work. The process is made even more time consuming and complex by an actor such as Jack, who has singular tastes in subject matter and who views his work not in terms of individual films but as a body, and who therefore strives for a variety and balance that gives his work a dimension not always apparent to others.

11

BEYOND STARDOM

Aside from a film's artistic and financial potential, another factor that influences his choice of projects is his view of film as a director's medium. He will sometimes choose a project solely for the opportunity of working with its director, and he does this for two reasons. The first is its benefit to him as an actor; he has claimed that his success as an actor is owing largely to the great directors he's worked with. The second reason is perhaps the most important for Jack: His desire to be a director is a consuming one that gnaws at him like an ulcer, and so in a sense he's secretly an apprentice director in every film he undertakes. For this reason, he seeks to work with the best; this was exemplified in his search for a film to follow *The Last Detail*.

There were two European productions in which he was very interested. One of them would have costarred Jeanne Moreau, but neither got into development. Then there was *The Great Gatsby*, which a friend, studio production chief Robert Evans, was developing at Paramount. Jack wanted to play Jay Gatsby, but according to Evans, he asked for more money than Paramount was prepared to pay. It was also reported that Jack didn't care for the way the project was being developed, and so he didn't push while negotiating for the picture. He also considered playing the role of Michael Corleone in *The Godfather*, because Marlon Brando had signed to do the film, but Jack turned it down. "I figured sooner or later Brando and I would do a film together," Jack said, "and I didn't want to blow it on one in which we'd have almost no scenes together."[2]

100

Jack turned down an opportunity to play a lead in *The Sting*, as well. He saw its commercial potential, but it didn't offer the kind of creative challenge he was looking for, and he passed it up for a more intriguing opportunity—a chance not only to work with the famous Italian director Michelangelo Antonioni but also to aid him professionally.

Antonioni had been having difficulty getting another project funded since his film *Zabriskie Point*, which was generally characterized as a disaster even by some of his most ardent followers. He had a film called *The Passenger*, which he wanted to do with Jack and Maria Schneider, whom Jack had known and dated long before she did *Last Tango in Paris* with Marlon Brando. Jack admired

Antonioni, regarding him as one of the best filmmakers. He would have welcomed the chance to work with the director under any circumstance, but when he learned that Antonioni could get funding for the film only if Jack signed to play the lead, he was all the more enthusiastic. "I did the movie totally because of Antonioni," he said. "He was having a tremendously difficult time . . . getting another film off, and this one couldn't have been done without my participation."[3]

The Passenger was filmed in Europe and Africa. Jack plays the part of David Locke, a political reporter on a television-documentary assignment who is so disillusioned and frustrated with his life that he assumes the identity of a man he has just met in a desert hotel. The Englishman who resembles him has died of natural causes in the room next to his. Locke exchanges papers with the dead man, whom he learns was a gun runner. With a female traveling companion whom he meets along the way (Schneider), he uses the dead man's appointment book to follow an itinerary that leads to his own death.

Antonioni was notorious for giving his actors little direction or motivation, and Jack was disappointed at how little give-and-take there was with the director. However, Nicholson liked Antonioni and out of respect gave the director exactly the performance he wanted. The chemistry between them was quite good. While Antonioni's intentionally anesthetic manner of storytelling usually depersonalizes his actors, Jack's presence gives this film a dimension that it would otherwise have lacked. As one critic pointed out about his performance, Jack, like Brando, has an "almost hypnotic gift of being absolutely present. As with Brando, it is almost impossible to take your eyes from him, even when he seems to be doing nothing."

The Passenger got relatively good reviews and made money, too, which pleased Jack. He liked the picture, and he particularly liked the fact that he had gotten along with the notoriously tempestuous director. "I mean, once you've been through a production with Michelangelo Antonioni, no one is going to ever throw you with strange moves, ever again," he said. "They tell me I'm the first actor in twenty-five years he got along with. But that was because I wanted to do an Antonioni movie, so if he wanted this kind of

101

performance I'm tickled to death to give it to him, tickled to death. Exactly what you see is *exactly* the performance he wanted, exactly."[4]

For his portrayal of David Locke, Jack was awarded the *Harvard Lampoon* Golden Thumbscrew Award for, in Jack's words, "proving once again that an actor can be successful playing an identity crisis."

While Jack was at work with Antonioni, an original screenplay that his old friend Robert Towne had written—a detective story called *Chinatown*—was wending a circuitous route through the production department at Paramount Pictures. Towne had developed the project as a vehicle he could employ to make his debut as a director, but nobody wanted to put such an expensive film in the hands of a new director. Therefore, he reluctantly sold the project to Robert Evans at Paramount, who signed Roman Polanski to direct it. Polanski was eager to take on *Chinatown* because it promised to be a big film, and he had not had a success since directing *Rosemary's Baby*.

Evans originally intended to cast his then wife, actress Ali McGraw, in the female lead, but when their marriage failed, he signed Faye Dunaway. Jack played Jake Gittes (whom Towne named after a friend of Jack's, producer Harry Gittes), a slick and cynical private detective in 1930s Los Angeles. Jack fashioned Gittes's appearance after that of his grandfather—a natty dresser; hair slicked back in the manner of the day—and for inspiration in the role, he also drew upon what he called a triangular offstage situation with actor-director John Huston, who portrayed the father of the woman with whom Gittes was having an affair. "I had just started going with John Huston's daughter," Jack said, "which the *world* might not have been aware of, but it could actually feed the moment-to-moment reality of my scene with him." Then Jack imitates John Huston's voice with a line from the film, " 'Are you sleeping with her?' "[5]

Though there are reminders throughout the film of the Chinese motif, only one scene takes place in Chinatown. The title represents a cultural warp, any gray area just beyond the law's grasp. We discover early in the film that Gittes was once a cop on the Chinatown beat and had learned that its inhabitants ran their own culture and that any outside interference brought only silence and shadows.

As a cop in a place like Chinatown, one's job was to do "as little as possible." It's an underground culture; it's only Chinatown.

As a private detective, Gittes spends most of his time shadowing cheating spouses—that is, until he gets involved in a case in which an executive with the city water authority is found drowned. He also discovers that although the city's in a drought, it's diverting water elsewhere. Feeling that this is somehow connected with the executive's death, he is drawn into the case. He's drawn in also by the dead man's widow, Mrs. Mulwray (Faye Dunaway), with whom he has an affair and who is obviously hiding something that Gittes suspects has to do with the water swindle. In fact, what Mrs. Mulwray is hiding is her daughter, a child she has had by her father, Noah Cross (Huston), who was the dead man's partner and who's searching for the child.

Eventually, Gittes unwittingly leads the father to the child—and to Mrs. Mulwray—but tries to arrange their escape, only to have the police tipped off and Mrs. Mulwray shot to death at their Chinatown rendezvous. Evil triumphs, and Gittes is consoled by a friend: "Forget it, Jake, it's only Chinatown."

There were spectacular fights on the set during the filming. They were usually between Polanski and Dunaway, because they didn't get along at all. Jack often acted as the mediator between them, but one day he and Polanski blew up on the set, as well. A Los Angeles Lakers basketball game was being televised and Jack was watching it between takes when Polanski, apparently feeling that Jack was paying more attention to the game than to the filming, is said to have struck the screen with a metal bar; the screen didn't explode, but Jack did. He and the director got into a heated altercation that ended with Jack ripping off his costume and both of them storming off the set in different directions. They later made up and have remained good friends, but Polanski learned that nobody comes between Jack Nicholson and his beloved Lakers.

Chinatown was an immense critical and financial success, and Jack's percentage deal eventually made him more than $1 million from the box-office receipts. It also proved to the industry, as producer Robert Evans pointed out, that Jack could carry leading-man roles as well as character roles. *Chinatown* drew a larger audience than any of Jack's other films, and Evans saw it as Jack's breakthrough picture, the one that transformed him from "an important critical star," with his coterie of fans, to a "major box-office star."[6]

Indeed, it was after *Chinatown* that Jack began getting the full Hollywood-star treatment—much to his delight. He became the 159th star invited to place his hand- and footprints in the forecourt of the Chinese Theatre in Hollywood. He was the subject of a *Time* magazine cover story. And writers began comparing him to Tracy, Bogart, and Cagney. He did not win an Oscar for *Chinatown* (Robert Towne did), but the big money and even bigger new reputation as one of the hottest stars in the business took some of the sting out of losing the Academy Award.

While *Chinatown* was in postproduction and the industry was looking at Jack from a more respectful perspective, he did a cameo in one film and costarred in another. The cameo was in *Tommy*, producer-director Ken Russell's equivalent of Bob Rafelson and Jack Nicholson's *Head;* it, too, was a Columbia release. *Tommy* is the screen version of the rock opera performed by The Who, and it starred them, along with Ann-Margret, Roger Daltry, Oliver Reed, and Elton John, among others. It's the story of a young Englishman who is psychologically stricken deaf, blind, and mute and who becomes a pop celebrity and is worshiped as the new messiah after defeating the Pinball Wizard (Elton John). Thematically, the opera deals with the absurdity of a culture that worships celebrity performers. The message is the medium in *Tommy*, and Russell mocks it accordingly, calling the film "the greatest artwork of the twentieth century." As with *Head*, most reviewers understood what the filmmakers were doing, but decided that it had been a wasted effort. Jack appeared—and did a little singing—as a medical doctor. He said he signed to do the picture because he thought it would be fun to work with its director, Ken Russell. He undoubtedly saw the *Head*-like, iconoclastic potential of the picture, as well. Then, too, it was an opportunity for him to work again with his *Carnal Knowledge* costar Ann-Margret, who did a very respectful turn in the picture despite the material. In any event, Jack apparently got what he wanted from the experience: He had fun making the film, and it did his career no harm.

After working with his *Carnal Knowledge* costar, Jack went to work once again with that picture's director, Mike Nichols, on *The*

104

Fortune, a project that had so many seductive elements that he couldn't have resisted it if he had tried. Besides having one of his favorite directors at the helm, the screenplay was written by his old friend Carol Eastman, it costarred his pal Warren Beatty, and it was a challenging comic part widely divergent from anything he had ever done. It's a 1920s story of two inept con men (Jack and Beatty) and a young heiress (Stockard Channing) whose fortune they try to gain through kidnapping, then through marriage, then, when all else fails, through murder. As the dim-witted partner of a dapper but equally bungling con man, Jack, with a perm resembling Art Garfunkel's hair style, turns in a very good performance—as do all the other cast members—but the picture slipped out of the studio almost unnoticed. It seemed to have everything going for it but an audience.

It was during the shooting of this picture that Jack learned the truth about his birth. The pursuant *Time* cover story and the success of *Chinatown* and of his next film not only overshadowed *Tommy* and *The Fortune* but also carried him beyond mere stardom.

"I think I may
have started a
few brush fires
in New York
that could burn
all the way
back to the
Coast."

Jack Nicholson[1]

12
MR.
BRANDO
AND
OTHER
PROBLEMS

In February 1975, after he had finished work on *The Fortune*, Jack went north to the Oregon State Mental Hospital at Salem, Oregon, the location site for his next film, *One Flew Over the Cuckoo's Nest*. He made the trip two weeks prior to the shooting in order to study the hospital routine and its patients in preparation for his part as a mental patient named Randle Patrick McMurphy. He spent several days mingling with the nonviolent patients on the wards, talking with them, playing parlor games with them, dining with them. Through observation windows, he studied the violent patients and observed their treatment—including electroshock therapy sessions, which McMurphy would be subjected to in the film. It was not unusual for Jack to take such painstaking efforts in preparation for a film role, especially one so far removed from his own experience. Meticulous preparation seemed particularly imperative for this role because its potential was enormous and he had therefore assumed it with reluctance and under self-imposed duress.

Cuckoo's Nest was based on the 1962 novel by author Ken Kesey and was coproduced by actor Michael Douglas, whose famous father, Kirk, had purchased the stage and screen rights and had starred in its 1963 Broadway dramatization. In the following decade, the elder Douglas tried unsuccessfully to bring the novel to the screen, but finally turned the rights over to his son. Michael Douglas and Saul Zaentz put the project together with United Artists and with a screenplay by Bo Goldman and Laurence Hauben. They chose Milos Forman to direct, owing to his often-demonstrated sensitivity at blending comedy and high drama. Louise Fletcher was cast as Nurse Ratched. Apparently, there was never a question about whom they wanted in the lead role.

Everyone connected with the project thought that Jack should play the part of Randle McMurphy, and all felt that he would be great in it. When their sentiments were made known to Jack, he considered turning the part down. He has always felt uncomfortable carrying what he called a "big reputation" into any film, and he was intimidated by the responsibility his peers would be inadvertently saddling him with if he signed for the part. Being good in the role, or even very good, would not be good enough.

It seemed to Jack an unintentional setup for a fall. If he committed to the film, he'd be assuming an obligation to deliver a great performance; it was expected of him. The obligation would be self-imposed, but the pressure would be no less intense. In the end, though, it was an offer he couldn't refuse. It was his kind of story, his kind of part, and the screenplay was excellent. He knew it would be an extraordinary film, and he couldn't resist the opportunity of working with Milos Forman. So he took the plunge.

One Flew Over the Cuckoo's Nest is the story of Randle Patrick McMurphy, a prison inmate who cons his way into a psychiatric hospital for ninety days of observation in an effort to evade the work details at a prison farm. Once on the ward, McMurphy befriends the inmates and sets out to improve the quality of their lives, revitalizing them by focusing on a common cause: rebelling against institutional bureaucracy as personified by Nurse Ratched. Ultimately, the institution destroys him.

It was a first-class production, and Jack enjoyed everything about it. Milos Forman was one of the few directors who wasn't put off by Jack's drawl, or impatient with his timing. Most would prompt him to speak faster—not Forman. "What I like most about Milos," Jack said, "is that the man has almost no tolerance for theatricality; he likes it actually real. If it's dull, fine."[2] Jack got along very well with Michael Douglas, too. Both men were trying to give up cigarette smoking and so they made a pact to stop. Whoever broke the pact first was to pay the other a thousand dollars. However, they were so adept at coaxing each other into moratoriums that the pact failed.

When the shooting wrapped, everyone thought they had an Academy Award contender. Jack felt he had met the challenge. Only time would tell how others viewed his performance. It would be months before the film was ready for release. In the meantime, he was concentrating on his next assignment, a Western called *The Missouri Breaks*, in which he would costar with Marlon Brando and on which principal photography had already begun on location about fifteen miles outside of Billings, Montana.

It was summer, and Jack's daughter, Jennifer, was on vacation from school, so he took her on location with him for a while. She was now twelve, old enough to appreciate the making of movies. The crew adopted her as one of their own, and she fit in so well that Jack had to admonish her for playing poker with them.

It was an isolated and relatively quiet location shoot, and when Jack wasn't busy with Jennifer during his time off, he did a lot of reading (the novel *Ragtime* among other things) and he granted an interview to writer Bill Davidson for *The New York Times Magazine*. The interview was conducted in his dressing-room trailer, and Davidson described how Jack watched Brando from the window as they talked. Brando was dressed in a yellow bathrobe and matching terry-cloth slippers and was scuttling back and forth between his own trailer and a pay phone, trying to resolve a union problem; a young photographer, a woman who was there on assignment for a women's magazine, had been banished from location, and Brando was trying to get her reinstated.

Jack was amused by Brando's intensity and admiring of his loyalty. Brando had reportedly spent most of the afternoon's shooting time on the telephone on the woman's behalf. Jack glanced at his watch.

"Oh, well," he said to Davidson, "another day, another twenty-one thousand dollars." Though he would eventually earn more than $1 million for his work in Chinatown, The Missouri Breaks was the first film on which he was guaranteed that amount; the shoot would last forty-seven and a half days, and Jack had prorated the amount he was earning daily. He was obviously pleased with this arrangement, but it was about the only aspect of the production that he found satisfactory.

Though Jack and Brando had been next-door neighbors for many years, they had had only a nodding acquaintance before they met on the location for The Missouri Breaks. Jack had always been eager to work with him, but as is often the case, the anticipation proved more savory than the event.

Brando arrived on location while Jack was still at work in Oregon. As the film's principal star (he was paid $1.5 million to Jack's $1 million), and in Jack's absence, he is reported to have exerted his influence with director Arthur Penn, expanding his own role (thereby minimizing Jack's) and making changes in the shooting schedule that enabled him to finish his part in the picture early, while Jack and the rest of the cast completed the shooting. In effect, Brando had stolen the film even before Jack arrived to begin shooting. "Poor Nicholson was stuck in the center of it all, cranking the damned thing out," Brando said, "while I whipped in and out of scenes like greased lightning."[3]

Always one to "serve the film," and to help make the filming as pleasant—or as nonconfrontational—as possible, Jack apparently didn't make an issue of Brando's tactics; he did let the director know that he thought the changes would hurt the film, would throw it "out of balance." Apparently no one dared to question Brando's wishes.

When it finally came time to shoot scenes with Brando and to watch him in action—which Jack had eagerly looked forward to doing—he was disappointed and disillusioned. He found doing scenes with him very difficult. Rather than memorize his lines, Brando read them from large cue cards held offcamera, making their scenes together feel mechanically contrived to Jack, rather than natural to play, which sorely tested his concentration. "Marlon's still the greatest actor in the world," Jack said, "so why does he need those goddamn cue cards?" To illustrate this point during his interview with Davidson, Jack moved his face very close to the writer's and had him look squarely into his eyes. As the writer did so, Jack's eyes wandered slowly off to the side, totally breaking the writer's concentration. "You see?" Jack said. "That's how it is doing a close scene with a guy who's looking at cue cards!"[4]

Jack was no closer to Brando when he finished working with him on the film than he had been from afar. Though cordial, they remained distant. Brando was distant from everyone. He stayed in his trailer most of the time, isolated from the cast and crew, or he rode a Honda trail bike alone over nearby mountain paths. Jack had hoped during the shoot to get Brando interested in working in a film he planned to direct, one that dealt thematically with the customs of the Pacific Northwest Indians. Brando had always had a consuming interest in the American Indian. But nothing came of Jack's plan. Whether Jack simply had given up on the idea after seeing Brando in action, or—more likely—whether Brando had turned him down or had wanted too much money to do the film isn't known. Jack would say only that after *The Missouri Breaks*, the possibility of Brando appearing in the film was closed to him.

Brando has always mocked everything that Jack takes seriously —movies, acting, the industry, the Oscars, the glamour, the adoration of fans. To Brando, the idea of adults playacting is frivolous; if someone wants to pay him lots and lots of money to do it, he will, but he still thinks it a childish business that should be kept in perspective. Jack had serious avenues to explore with Brando, but all he got from the "greatest actor in the world" were jokes for answers.

Even after the film was released, Jack still was getting backlash from working with Brando. The entertainment press began asking him about an allusion Brando was said to have made in an Italian interview about his having a homosexual affair with Jack. Nicholson refused to comment. He wasn't aware of what Brando had said, exactly, but he knew that it wasn't true and that it had been either made up or was what he called a "circular quote," meaning one that is misinterpreted or taken out of context and printed as fact, and then so often and widely reprinted that it comes to be presumed as fact whether or not it's denied.

The fact was that Brando's comment was in answer to a specific question posed by a member of the Italian press. The interviewer had somehow inferred from the *Missouri Breaks* story line that the relationship of the characters portrayed by Jack and Brando in the film was a homosexual one. He asked Brando about this, and what Brando actually said was, "If there is someone who is convinced that Jack Nicholson and I are lovers [as characters] in this film, may they continue to do so. I find it amusing." He was then cited as having alluded to an affair between the actors rather than the characters. "Those circular quotes can kill you," Jack said.[5]

With an $8 million budget, Arthur Penn directing, and Marlon Brando and Jack Nicholson starring, *The Missouri Breaks* had to be great. The critics and moviegoers expected it to be great. It wasn't. It was interesting but too disjointed and episodic to come anywhere near its potential. Jack thought it could have been saved in the editing, but his opinion was disregarded. He didn't like the film, and he told director Penn so. According to Jack, Penn was offended and stopped speaking to him.

Jack was tired after the filming. He had done seven movies in two years. He needed time off from acting, and he wanted to try his hand at directing again. He would have done so directly after finishing *Breaks* had he not been offered a chance to work with director Elia Kazan.

Though he was generally against doing cameo roles in all-star films, the kind that list the cast alphabetically, he made an exception for *The Last Tycoon*, a screen adaptation of F. Scott Fitzgerald's unfinished novel. He did so because Kazan's custom of doing that kind of film made it seem more professionally acceptable and less a star cattle call. Jack played a Communist union organizer in the film, and had only a couple of scenes, so he was able to do it quickly and in time to begin the domestic promotion tour for *Cuckoo's Nest*, which he was committed to do. Anjelica also had a small role in the Kazan film, but she had no scenes with Jack and so was still at work on it when he went on tour.

His promotion tour began in New York City in the fall of 1975. He and Anjelica had gotten along splendidly, and he had been on his best behavior for more than a year. Being in New York alone, however, was too great a temptation. He went on a "skunk"-chasing binge that lasted nearly a week and that included among his prey at least two fashion models, one of whom Anjelica had considered a friend. Owing to the fashion world's closed circuitry, word of his activities was relayed to Anjelica by week's end. Fearing as much, and still on tour, Jack boarded a plane for Chicago, telling a friend, "I think I may have started a few brush fires in New York that could burn all the way back to the Coast."

Anjelica had been totally devoted to Jack, and she was very hurt. She had suffered such goings-on as a child: Her father had been as indiscreet in his affairs, which had eventually broken up the family. She was also deeply humiliated that Jack had chosen to forage in her old stomping ground and among her former professional peers. She knew that he must have known word would get back to her. If this was a signal from him, she could send signals of her own. She began an affair with another Irish actor with a dazzling smile, Ryan O'Neal, who, not incidentally, also happened to be a friend of Jack's (and whom, reportedly, Jack has never forgiven).

Jack was still on tour when she had the affair. He is said to have learned about it from the gossip columns. "Jack was slammed hard by the Ryan O'Neal thing," a friend was quoted as saying. "I guess he really does have a double standard about fidelity."[6] Jack said almost ten years later, "I didn't blame her in the beginning. I didn't like it [the affair], but I think being my girlfriend has so many things even I couldn't deal with that I can honestly say I don't blame her, although I was hurt."[7]

Anjelica had moved into an apartment of her own in Beverly Hills by the time Jack returned from his tour. Her affair with O'Neal was brief, however, so it wasn't long before she was back with Jack in the house on Mulholland Drive, under a wary truce. It was their first major battle and separation, but it wouldn't be their last.

A few months later, in the spring of 1976, Jack was back in New York City—this time with Anjelica—for a brief stopover on his way abroad for a vacation and to promote the European distribution of *Cuckoo's Nest*. Since he had learned in the early days with Corman that theatrical makeup blotted out his eyebrows and made him look badly, Jack has refused to wear it and takes what he calls a "reverse narcissistic" pride in that fact. His one exception is a technique he learned from Warren Beatty of applying makeup to the hairline, which absorbs harsh studio light, thereby stopping the reflective glare that would otherwise make thinning hair seem to disappear. This technique necessitates having a hairline with which to work, and Jack's was receding fast. Therefore, he stopped in

New York City to be treated by Dr. Norman Orentreich, known as the "father of the hair transplant," and with an assortment of hats to protect the new growth, he and Anjelica departed for Europe.

Jack spent several weeks promoting *Cuckoo's Nest* and then vacationed for a while on the French Riviera aboard producer Sam Spiegel's yacht. He was definitely unwinding. He is said to have gotten embroiled with a waiter in St. Tropez—perhaps because he refused to remove his hat—and while seeing the sights, he was hounded by a horde of camera-carrying locals until he retreated to the marina and Spiegel's yacht, where he reportedly tried to discourage the mob with choice Anglo-Saxonisms. When that tack failed, he resorted to what one magazine called "international sign language": He dropped his trousers and mooned the multitudes.[8]

From the Riviera, Jack and Anjelica went to London for more rest and relaxation and a round of parties before returning to the United States to attend the Academy Award ceremonies. Jack had been nominated by the Academy of Motion Picture Arts and Sciences for an award as Best Actor for his role in *One Flew Over the Cuckoo's Nest*. It was his fifth nomination, and while he again thought he had a chance to win, he braced himself for the possibility of losing by lamenting publicly that he wasn't the kind of actor for whom the Academy voted, because of his lifestyle and because he wasn't involved in charities and the like. In speaking of his losses in four previous Oscar nominations, he said, "The only man I deserved to lose to was George C. Scott in *Patton*."[9] This time he won, however, and he took unabashed delight in accepting the Oscar. Afterward, he said, "I was beginning to think I'd have to die and get an Oscar posthumously. Winning it is like making love for the first time—once you've done it, you don't have to worry about it ever again."[10]

In fact, the evidence suggests that being an Oscar winner was more a curse than a blessing.

1963 — Jack and then-wife, Sandra Knight, in a scene from *The Terror,* the only film they made together. Sandra retired from acting after this picture was made.

1962 — Supporting player Jack Nicholson in a scene from his sixth film, *The Broken Land*, with the film's co-star, Dianna Darrin.

1969 — Dennis Hopper, Peter Fonda, and Jack in a scene from
Easy Rider, the film that made Jack a star after he had given up acting for directing.

1971 — Art Garfunkel, Candice Bergen, and Jack as college youths in *Carnal Knowledge*.
During the making of this film, Jack spent weekends editing
his first directorial effort, *Drive, He Said.*

1974 — Jack with his *Chinatown* co-star
Faye Dunaway.

c. 1971 — Jack with Michelle Phillips,
who was his constant companion
until she left him for Warren Beatty.
Jack's mustache was for his
role in *A Safe Place*.

1970 — Jack with daughter Jennifer, age 6, by his former wife, Sandra Knight.

1974 — Anjelica Huston's half-sister, Allegra, age 11, Jack's daughter Jennifer, age 11, Jack, and Anjelica on the pool deck of Jack's Mulholland Drive home.

1974 — Jack as former cop turned private detective
Jake Gittes in *Chinatown*.

1974 — Jack in his Academy Award–winning performance as Randle Patrick McMurphy in *One Flew Over the Cuckoo's Nest.* He considered turning down the film because everyone expected him to be great in the role.

1976 — Producer-actor Michael Douglas, director Milos Foreman, actress Louise Fletcher, Jack, and producer Saul Zaentz pose with the Oscars they were awarded for their work on *One Flew Over the Cuckoo's Nest.*

1977 — Jack and Anjelica Huston at an American Film Institute function in
Los Angeles. Anjelica had retired from modeling
and would not begin her acting career for another four years.

1980 — Jack as would-be writer Jack Torrance in a scene from *The Shining*, filmed in London.

1980 — Jack in a scene from *The Shining*, a role he took in order to work with director Stanley Kubrick and to satisfy a need to break from his usual naturalistic acting style.

1981 — Jack and Jessica Lange in a scene from *The Postman Always Rings Twice*, which was more successful abroad than in the United States.

1985 — Shirley MacLaine and Jack in a scene from *Terms of Endearment*, for which both won Oscars.

1981 — Actor Orson Welles with Jack at a tribute given for Welles by the Hollywood Foreign Press Association at the Beverly Hilton Hotel in Los Angeles. Welles was one of four elder mentors whom Jack held in high esteem.

1976 — Marlon Brando and Jack in a scene from *The Missouri Breaks*. Though Jack had always wanted to work with Brando, he found doing it a very trying experience.

Jack in one of his frequent trips abroad. This was taken in London
at about the time he made *The Shining*.

1984 — During time off while filming *Prizzi's Honor* in New York City, Jack traveled by limousine to visit one of his childhood haunts, the boardwalk at Asbury Park, New Jersey.

1985 — A publicity still for *Prizzi's Honor*: Jack, Kathleen Turner, director John Huston, and Anjelica Huston.

1987 — Stars of *The Witches of Eastwick*,
clockwise: Jack, Michelle Pfeiffer, Susan Sarandon, and Cher.

c. 1988 — Jack with former Senator and Mrs. Gary Hart and actor-director
Warren Beatty. Jack actively campaigned for Hart in the former Senator's ill-fated bids to
become his party's nominee as a Presidential candidate.

1988 — Former
heavyweight
boxing champion
Muhammad Ali
with Jack at the
Trump Plaza in
New York City.

1989 — Michael Keaton and Jack in a scene from *Batman*. Jack told Keaton, "Ya gotta let the wardrobe do the acting, kid."

1989 — Jack as the Joker in *Batman*, the film that made him, in his own words, "extremely financially viable"; his earnings from the film are estimated at between $30 and $60 million.

1990 — Ruben Blades, Paul A. DiCocco, Jr., and Jack in a scene from *The Two Jakes.*

1990 — Jack as private detective Jake Gittes in *The Two Jakes*, the *Chinatown* sequel that Jack also directed.

13 THE CURSE OF ANSWERED PRAYERS

It was just seven years after the time of his discovery in *Easy Rider* that Jack was awarded the highest honor of the Motion Picture Academy of Arts and Sciences, an honor that most actors aspire to and even dream of but that few receive. Even though Jack intellectually subscribed to the view that all tributes are false and all is vanity, he apparently also views such awards as symbolic of belonging, of acceptance into the family of filmmakers, and so the emotional side of him takes a wondrous delight in the Oscars and in the glamour and fame that attend them. There was, however, a somber side to the achievement.

Seven years also had passed since he had expressed the desire to quit acting and since his realization that it is the creative and not the performing province of filmmaking that excites him most and that gives him a greater sense of fulfillment than acting, alone, can provide. Part of the fulfillment is in the creative processes itself, in the writing, directing, editing, and producing. Beyond the process is something else: the degree of *control* over the final product that one exercises in directing and producing. To Jack, for whom restraint is anathema, the need for control over all aspects of his life is a compulsive one.

This need was evident early on, when even as a young boy in New Jersey he reached the understanding with his family that he had taken sole charge of his life and that he required a minimum of guidance and expected no interference. It is also displayed by his extreme possessiveness, which embodies this desire to control. Losing control of possessions that to others might seem of little importance can very nearly incapacitate him. He's possessive of the women in his life and would like to have them all back under his roof—and in his control; the loss of a girlfriend can drive him to deep despair. Even the temporary loss or misplacement at home of things such as his billfold or car keys causes him fits of frenzy that are said to be unnerving to behold. So it seems logical that his need for control would extend to filmmaking, as well.

When stardom changed his course from directing, Jack saw the diversion as temporary; he was eager to capitalize on his new celebrity but determined not to be sidetracked by it. His subsequent failure to gain a position of authority as a director with *Drive, He Said* prompted him to react as he usually did when a prized possession slipped from his grasp. He grew angry, demoralized, and terribly depressed. His suggestion that he had not directed as much as he wanted to because he couldn't resist the million-dollar acting offers he was getting, while undoubtedly true, appears to be a rationalization. He knew he should climb back on the horse that threw him, but what little confidence he had had in his ability to direct was so badly shaken that he could only back away from the experience. "One of the things I have to overcome as a director," he said, "is that it's very hard for me to find a place to put my individual foot down where I don't know how one of the masters does it already."[2] Rather than risk the possibility of failure again, he redoubled his effort to work with and learn from the best directors.

Many stars try from their positions as actors to exercise power with regard to their films. They attempt to influence producers. They demand rewrites of scripts. They question or challenge the

116

authority and decisions of directors. It wasn't Jack's nature to resort to such tactics, and even if it had been, he knew that such control was merely symbolic and that it usually resulted only in harming the film and giving the actor a bad reputation in the business. If he was trapped by circumstance in a subordinate filmmaking role —and by allowing years to lapse before again attempting to direct, and by losing the incentive and discipline to write (though not the desire), he was, indeed, accepting a subordinate role—then he was determined to make the best of it by exercising control over his craft, and thereby serving the film. Above all, Nicholson is the consummate professional.

To this end, Jack further developed methods for improving his acting skills, and he adopted theories that at once gave him the inspiration and incentive to continue acting while at the same time rationalized his temporary abandonment of writing and directing. "I consider what I do to be writing in a very modern sense," he said of his acting. "The modern writer is the screen actor. Acting is action writing, like Jackson Pollack is an action painter. And I made the decision kind of like this thing about action writing. I thought, well, if I'm right about what I can do as an actor, I've got to relax my own desires to direct, because I can be a vehicle for a lot of directors. That's my job. I augment. And in that way I may be contributing more."[3] He was, of course, "relaxing his desires to direct" under duress, and so he augmented.

He has always been analytical and methodical in his approach to acting. Director Arthur Penn alluded to this when he contrasted Jack's approach to Marlon Brando's. According to Penn, Brando feels the drift of a scene and goes with it. Nicholson is more organized, Penn says; he knows where he wants to go, while Brando apparently doesn't want to know where he's going. Like Brando and James Dean, Jack also is said to have learned that hidden feelings used in the portrayal of a role (what is felt but not overtly expressed on camera) can sometimes have as great an effect on a portrayal as overt expressions. To this end, he uses what he calls "secrets" in every role he plays. His secrets may have form, such as props, which invoke in him a mood or attitude that helps motivate him in a manner not apparent to his audience, or they may be intangible "secrets," such as real-life circumstances that help form an internal dynamic to drive a portrayal or an emotional moment. He has cited numerous examples of both, but typical of the latter would be his portrayal of Bobby Dupea in *Five Easy Pieces* as an allegory of his own career, or playing Randle McMurphy in *Cuckoo's Nest* as a man who is irresistible to women and who thinks he can and will seduce the ward nurse—which neither happens nor is suggested in the film. Examples of props as "secrets" are his use of eyeglasses like John Nicholson's in his portrayal of George Hanson, the personable alcoholic in *Easy Rider,* and the poem he describes as "extremely revealing" that he wrote expressly for Diane Keaton and handed to her oncamera in his portrayal of playwright Eugene O'Neill in *Reds.*

Jack's approach to a role begins with the script itself, which he annotates with questions and observations. He even treats his passages of dialogue as a musical score, ascribing beats to the words and pauses, each beat representing the measure of time he'll take in delivering words, phrases, or pauses. His interpretation of the characters he portrays is analytical, as well. "I work very personally," he says, "their [the characters'] behavior [patterns] are an extension of my behavior. . . . I always try to translate them into characters with a positive philosophy. In other words, I try to feel that what they're doing is the right thing."[4]

We seldom see ourselves as others do, and that's the way Jack portrays the characters he plays. "You have to search out and adopt the character's own justifications and rationalizations," he says. He doesn't play stereotypes, and he tries not to play the obvious quality or emotion that the script seems to call for or that an audience might expect. "In acting," he has said, "it's best when you don't really know. Unpredictability is the most arresting quality that an actor can have; it's as important to an actor as color-sense and line are to a painter."[5] Rather than play the quality, Jack tries to react the way he thinks the character would react. An example of this would be the crying scene in *Five Easy Pieces* that caused a disagreement between him and director Bob Rafelson. The director wanted him to play the quality—to be moved to tears—and Jack was not inclined to do so. In this instance, though, he trusted Rafelson's instinct over his own, and his trust proved to be well placed.

He also strives to avoid using his offcamera persona in his characterizations, the physical mannerisms and personality traits that he developed to ingratiate himself with others and that he knows please his audience and that have a guaranteed, endearing effect on them. In short, he refrains from using all the qualities he used in *Easy Rider* that won him an audience and that established him as both distinctive and familiar in the tradition of stars like Henry Fonda and Spencer Tracy: the disarming smile, the urbane, self-assured attitude that writer Stephen Schiff described as "a magnetic complicity with the audience, a way of assuring the viewer that he is more aware, more in on the joke than the plodders around him—and that we could be too if we'd only join him."[6] Such comments have at times made Jack almost phobic in his efforts to avoid using these known qualities.

Jack often refers to his fans as his "constituency," and by implication, he's the outsiders' representative, their ambassador to Hollywood—the one through whom they can experience vicariously the glamour of it all. His attitude therefore seems to have a tacit subtext: "Heeey, *look* at us! Are you kiddin'? We're in a movie here, for crissakes! We're hobnobbin' with the stars up here on the silver screen—makin' a mil—and they don't even know what we're *doin'* up here, ya know what I mean?" It was an attitude to which critic John Simon referred in speaking of Jack's early career: "One cannot get around the feeling that the basic pigment of all Nicholson performances is an impasto of smugness."[7]

But Jack changed that. Soon writers such as Brad Darrach were saying of him, "Even when he acts, Nicholson closely restrains his expressions. Mystery is at the heart of his art; the spectator can only guess what goes on behind the features on the screen. . . . In effect, [he] has become a realist/ironist who assumes a wary attitude toward the fairly desperate characters he portrays. . . . In art as in life, one never quite knows which way this cat is jumping, and that's the way he likes it."[8] It is not only the way he likes it, but the way it must be with him. He has a genuine horror of being predictable and therefore known, what he calls a "gypsy fear" of losing the magic. "My style of acting is to try to do something different each time," he says, "as long as I can afford it."[9]

Winning the Oscar was a turning point. Jack made a craft decision, a conscious effort to change his acting style, and this puzzled critics and fans alike. He may have been leaning toward change in any event, but for an actor like Jack—who plots his every career move like a battlefield general—being named Best Actor certainly fixed his position and made him vulnerable. The spotlight would be more intense and the audience more demanding. He would no longer be the outsider who surprised. He'd be carrying more of the dreaded baggage of a star, *expected* to carry pictures with his presence. He had nearly turned down the role that won him the Oscar because the director and producer expected him to be great in the part. Now, as an Oscar winner, wouldn't *everyone* expect him to be great in *every* part? Was this his motivation for change? Or was it because he now considered the acting style that had won him the Oscar a guaranteed quality? Or was it because the Oscar had a liberating effect? Perhaps he felt he had established his credentials and had earned the right to experiment with style.

Whatever the reason, his change was a conscious one. "I wanted to be bigger," he said. "I wanted to attempt the affectation of style within cinematic acting, which is something the audience heavily penalizes you for because they're stuck at the turn of the century; they're only interested in naturalism. I was trying to set a new standard for myself . . . pushing at the modern edges of acting. My work changed 'cause I thought it was harder to do—I *know* it's harder to do; it's just *harder* to do."[10]

Jack used his new acting style in at least his next two films—some say three. It amounted to, or resulted in, sweeping histrionics and overly broad characterizations. Judging from the reaction of critics and many fans, the effect wasn't good.

Jack had worked for two years straight on six films in three countries by the time he finished *Cuckoo's Nest* in the fall of 1975. He needed time to "lay back and let the juices flow," he said. He was also concerned that his image had been up on the screen too often in those two years and that while his audience might not be satiated, it was probably not eagerly anticipating the next Jack Nicholson movie, either. And that, as he would say, wasn't good for business. So it was a good time to give acting a rest and a good opportunity to rejuvenate himself by exercising the creative urges to write and direct that nagged at him. Toward this end, he spent the winter at Aspen, Colorado, on a working vacation, skiing and putting the finishing touches to his own screen adaptation of Donald Barry's mystical novel *Moontrap*. Set in Oregon in the 1850s, *Moontrap*

14

OVER THE TOP

is the story of an old mountain man who once had lived with a Pacific Northwest Indian tribe and in the mountains had raised a boy who was later integrated into white society. Close to death, the old man feels beholden to the spiritual mystique of his adopted tribe, which dictates that one must be hunted by one's own people when death is near. So he calls upon the young man to carry out the mystical rite.

Moontrap was the project in which Jack tried to cast Brando. He had owned the film rights for several years before getting the financial backing to coproduce and direct it. After spending the winter preparing it for production, however, the backers apparently violated the spirit if not the letter of their agreement with him by stipulating at the last minute that he could direct the film only if he appeared in it—a condition that Jack wouldn't accept. Reluctantly, he abandoned the project, hoping one day to do the film the way he thinks it ought to be done.

Jack also had an arrangement with Paramount Pictures to direct and star in a film. He had hoped to reenter the film directors' ranks with a substantial effort, but he had also committed to play the lead in Stanley Kubrick's *The Shining,* to be filmed in England. The time he had lost working on *Moontrap* precluded his searching for another project, so he settled for *Goin' South,* a comedy-Western he had previously optioned and that had a role he wanted to play. Besides the time factor, his decision also was based partly on his desire to simplify the task of directing; a comedy-Western was not nearly as complex to handle as a film such as *Drive, He Said.*

Goin' South is a romantic comedy, coauthored by Jack's friend from his acting-school days, John Shaner. It's set in the post–Civil War West and concerns Henry Moon (Jack), a ne'er-do-well former cook with Quantrill's raiders. Like many in his former group, Moon couldn't or wouldn't fit back into society at war's end, and he turned bank robber and horse thief and ends up jailed in Longhorn, Texas, about to be hanged. His girlfriend, Hermine, and the motley members of his old gang visit his cell bearing bad news: They don't want to risk trying to rescue him. The lovers' tearful farewell is exemplary of the film's tone: "You're the best I ever had," Hermine says to the condemned Henry Moon, " 'Cept maybe that circus fella." Later in the film, Moon pays her his highest compliment: "You was the first woman I didn't have to pay for," he says.

122

Longhorn's bachelor population has been decimated by the Civil War; to compensate, there's a town law that any man sentenced to be hanged for any offense except murder can be spared from the gallows if a townswoman chooses to marry him. And so Henry Moon is saved just as the noose is being placed around his worthless neck; he's chosen on impulse by a pretty young woman named Julia Tate (Mary Steenburgen). Moon thinks he has lived and gone to heaven until he learns that theirs is a marriage in name only; she has chosen him out of need for a strong back to work the meager gold mine her father left her. *Goin' South* is a simple and amusing tale with no surprises; eventually Henry and Julia discover one another and discover gold, as well.

Jack reportedly wanted to cast Jane Fonda as Julia, but that couldn't be arranged. He tested Jessica Lange for the part but instead chose Mary Steenburgen, a talented and unknown young actress who had never worked in motion pictures. "I did a screen test," Steenburgen said, "and when I hadn't heard anything five days later I was going to go back to New York. I went to Paramount to get the money they owed me for my hotel bill, and Jack was sitting there, smoking a big cigar, and he said, " 'Don't worry about it. You're on the payroll.' "[2]

Paramount bridled at Jack's casting a newcomer to costar with him, but he was adamant and was later not only delighted with her work in the film but happy to have given her the opportunity. "Mary had never even been in a movie studio," he said. "I do feel gratified because she's an unusual actress, and without that break it might have taken her years before her talent was recognized. I feel I saved her from all that."

"When I won the Oscar [Best Supporting Actress, 1980] for *Melvin and Howard*," Steenburgen said, "I thanked Jack in my [acceptance] speech, though he had nothing to do with that film. I said if anybody ever had a patron saint . . . Then I said how, in 1977, when he insisted on casting me in *Goin' South* everybody told him he was crazy. Well, I said, thank goodness for me that he was."[3]

Also in the cast were Christopher Lloyd and Danny DeVito, both of whom appeared in *Cuckoo's Nest* and later gained national prominence in the television series "Taxi." In addition to Steenburgen, there were two other members of the cast without movie experience:

Jack's brother-in-law, George W. "Shorty" Smith, was one. Shorty had a nonspeaking role as Mr. Anderson, one of four people who come to call on the newlywed Moons. The other newcomer was "Saturday Night Live" television star John Belushi, who appeared as a deputy sheriff.

Goin' South was filmed in Durango, Mexico, from mid-August through late October 1977. Durango is a small city on the fertile interior plateau of the Sierra Madre in northern Mexico, about five hundred miles northwest of Mexico City, famed for its beauty and favored by filmmakers as a Western location cite. Jack rented a large house in the foothills that often was used by filmmakers; it was designed with comfortable living quarters and with separate offices and editing and screening rooms. He settled in and the shoot was relatively uneventful until John Belushi arrived.

Like many of the "Saturday Night Live" performers, Belushi had been discovered while working on the television show. He was under contract to do a feature role in the film *Animal House* when Jack's producer approached him to portray a Mexican deputy sheriff in *Goin' South*. It was a bit part that Jack thought Belushi would probably turn down, but he was flattered to be asked; he admired Jack and had done impressions of him in comedy skits. He also thought it a good opportunity to gain experience in film work before starting *Animal House*. By the time he got to Durango, however, it was apparent that he had had second thoughts about doing the film.

124   Jack's rented house was the check-in point for arriving cast and crew members. When Belushi arrived, he announced to the location-office help that he wanted to go home. The cast and crew were shooting on location, but word that he was there and causing trouble was relayed to the location site by two-way radio, and coproducer Harold Schneider drove up to the house to see what the problem was. Belushi was in a highly agitated state when Schneider arrived. He said he didn't like his hotel; he didn't like the location; and he didn't like the whole idea of doing the film. He was arrogant and rude. They were in the kitchen, and while pacing and ranting, Belushi pulled a knife from a drawer and fingered it menacingly—as though he might do harm to Schneider or himself. Schneider spent two or three hours with him, mostly listening and trying to understand what was really troubling him, but Belushi just

ranted on, repeating himself. When the other producer, Harry Gittes, arrived, he took over and listened for a while, too, until Belushi finally fell asleep.

Eventually, Jack returned from location. It was late and he was tired from the day's shooting; he had never met the young TV performer, and he was not inclined to put up with the kind of marathon session that Belushi had put his producers through, so he told them to wake Belushi up and get him back to his hotel. Belushi insisted on seeing Jack but was told that he hadn't returned from location. He apparently didn't believe this and got into a shoving match with the producers that almost came to blows before members of the crew intervened, separating the combatants and sending Belushi on his way.

Belushi was vulnerable at the time; he apparently felt insecure. He had traveled to Mexico alone, leaving his wife, friends, and familiar surroundings. He was in a strange country, working with strangers, among strangers, on his own, and he had never worked on a film before. He also may have felt that the small part he had agreed to do wasn't worth the inconvenience and stress it was causing him. Had he expressed this with more coherence, rather than trying to intimidate his way out of his commitment, the production executives might have been more disposed to help him through his problems. Instead, he was sullen, demanding, and aggressive, pronouncing everything, in his words, "suck-o" and wanting out. The producers had no time to recast the part, and to them he seemed intent on sabotaging the production to satisfy his ego. Indeed, he later bragged to the makeup man, who had not witnessed the scuffling, that he had "hit the producer," which was not true.

Belushi apologized the following day, but Schneider, who had wasted an evening and almost had come to blows with him, was not inclined to forget or forgive Belushi's arrogance. Jack was cordial to him but kept his distance; he had brought his cook down to Mexico with him and he often gave dinner parties for those in his inner circle, but Belushi was made to understand that he was to show up there only when invited.

Eventually, Belushi's wife joined him in Durango and he finished the shooting, which was thereafter relatively quiet, though there were still minor problems. Owing to the temperature extremes, Belushi caught walking pneumonia, and Jack fractured his hand

125

and injured several ribs when he was thrown from his horse, but such incidents caused only slight delays, and the picture was wrapped in late October, slightly over schedule.

Jack was still editing the film when Belushi went back to the West Coast to do his third film, *Old Boyfriends*—he had finished *Animal House* several months after *Goin' South* had wrapped. Jack needed Belushi to dub a couple of lines on the sound track, so he had Schneider call Belushi's agent. Although Belushi was in town and the dubbing would have taken only about twenty minutes of his time—and although such minor work ordinarily would have been done free as a courtesy to the producer—the agent reportedly was upset with what he perceived to be the ill treatment of his client in Mexico. He therefore insisted that Schneider furnish Belushi a car and driver and give him one hundred dollars for expenses. This was a negligible expense in the multimillion-dollar production, but Jack and Schneider took offense on principle. It's said that Jack became angry and dubbed the lines himself, imitating Belushi's voice, but on further thought, however, Jack decided that if his action became known, it could result in union problems. He had no alternative other than to bring Belushi back.

In what appeared to be a vindictive spirit, Schneider sent out to the bank for one hundred dollars in coins and made arrangements for the smallest automobile on the Paramount lot—a compact—to be sent for Belushi, with a woman driver; presumably all three—the payment in coins, the small car, and the woman driver—were considered instruments of disrespect. Belushi arrived and did the dubbing quickly. When he finished, Schneider paid him with the bag of coins. Belushi went straight to his agent's office from the studio, where he burst into tears of humiliation. The agent was incensed. He reported the incident to Paramount, then sent a telegram to Schneider, complaining of his conduct. Schneider is said to have tacked the telegram up on his wall.[4]

Though Schneider is alleged to be the one who ordered the actions against Belushi—with the knowledge of coproducer Harry Gittes—the *Goin' South* production was Jack's show, and no one could do anything like that without his knowledge and consent. Belushi knew this, and for a long time railed against Jack whenever his name was mentioned, vowing to punch him if he ever saw him again. But in time, and after Belushi proved himself in films, they became friends, and Jack took a fraternal interest in him, advising him in career matters.

Goin' South was released in October of 1978. Worried about how he would be received as a director, Jack spent an inordinately long time editing. But for all of his added effort, the film made a modest showing. It was met with audience indifference, with little critical approval, and with no unqualified praise. Jack later said of this second directorial effort, "I had that sense of signature . . . 'Okay, I don't have any undone job that I didn't get time to do.' Wherever there were choices, you know, I made more good ones than bad ones, and where I made bad ones, I made more good adjustments to deal with that, and so forth. And the movie simply was not received that way. . . . I feel talented as a director. I don't feel *desired* as a director, because there I don't believe in the craft separate from the audience. If they don't like the movie, that's it, that's what a movie's about. Doesn't mean *I* don't think it's good."[5]

Jack also lamented that critics failed to recognize the serious subtext of the film: The failure of the United States' first guerrilla warriors to fit back into society. However, the fact is that what Jack perceived as a subtext—Henry Moon's dilemma as a victim of circumstance—came off as a simple and inconsequential plot device. The reason for this goes back to the craft decisions he had made just prior to doing *Goin' South*. He had decided to direct again, then had decided to direct himself (though the decision was made under duress) at a time when he had determined to broaden his acting style. As a result, he played Henry Moon as a leering, tongue-darting Gabby Hayes with teeth, snuffling and snorting, shuffling and scratching—with no director to keep him from going over the top with his characterization. Comedy or not, the audience apparently wasn't ready for a love story between Mary Steenburgen and Gabby Hayes, and Jack's broad, farcical treatment precluded or overshadowed any suggestion of a subtle subtext.

This is not to say that *Goin' South* is a bad motion picture. Jack designed it as entertainment, and that's what he delivered. It's funny, entertaining, and highly underrated. It's also well directed. It was a disappointment to many who saw it, however, probably because they expected more of Jack Nicholson. So it was Jack himself and not so much his film, that was reviewed. As he had feared, his "big reputation" was being factored into the critiques of his work. Many of his "constituents" hated his "bigger" acting style; so did most critics, who also chastized him as a director for not reining in his own self-indulgent acting. There was another factor involved. Industry insiders were alleging a heavy use of cocaine on location during the filming. Several reviewers were obviously influenced by such insider talk, and there were numerous not-so-subtle allusions to drug use in reviews, particularly with respect to Jack's peculiar and bothersome nasal intonation throughout the film (which Jack insists was a glottal voice—like that of Clark Gable —that he cultivated for the role). To some, this seemed to explain why his acting had gotten suddenly so peculiar. One critic said he acted with the abandon of "a mime on an acid trip."[6] Another referred to his "somewhat stoned eyes,"[7] another to his "peculiar nasal voice and fogged manner."[8]

In defense, Jack reiterated that he had purposefully changed his acting style and that two of the films in question—*Goin' South,* a farce, and *The Shining,* a horror film—did not lend themselves to his usual naturalistic style. In alluding to the rumor of drugs affecting his performance in *Goin' South,* Jack pointed out to one interviewer that as the director of the picture, he could have dubbed the entire sound track if the glottal quality had been unintentional. The reviewer wrote: ". . . it is hard not to feel put-on. There is probably no way of getting at the truth of it." He continued: "There is, whether it's true or not, a fairly accepted view in the business that they [drugs] have a lot to do with his performances, a view exacerbated by his odd-voiced nasality in *Goin' South.*"[9]

"I gave this great press conference in Europe . . . and all they wrote about was cocaine, which I didn't even say *anything* about!"

Jack Nicholson[1]

A uthor David Thomson once wrote an essay about Jack that began with a fragment of a parable. The time is the future, and among the notable archaeological digs is one that is located a few miles northwest of what had been the city of Los Angeles. Found at the site was the fossilized imprint of a twentieth-century male, whom archaeologists named Mulholland Man. Several fossilized imprints of females—in postures of abandon—were found with him in the rubble of what appeared to be a "pleasuring room" of his dwelling on a low mountain range that had overlooked the city. Judging from fragments of awards and other artifacts subsequently found, the archaeologists determined that Mulholland Man was a thespian who bore the name Jack Nicholson. A curious aspect of the find was the outline of his fossilized

15

MULHOLLAND

MAN

imprint: It was nearly luminous from a compound composed of volcanic dust and cocaine.[2]

The parable is illustrative of a common perception about Jack. Ask people what they think of when his name is mentioned, and drugs will be among their first associations. It's illustrative, too, of the way writers often deal with the perception. Nicholson has come to loathe such allusions.

What seems to bother Jack most is not the perception itself but the fact that it detracts from his promotional efforts, interferes with the marketing of his work. He complains that when he talks to interviewers, they always want to know and write about his use of drugs. If this is so, there are two reasons. One is that since the late 1970s, he has refused to give personal interviews regarding his private life; about the only time he'll grant them is when he has something to sell—when he's promoting his latest film. Since his promotion tours are the only times most reporters get to ask him questions, it's small wonder that they take advantage of such rare opportunities. Another reason that the press asks about drugs is owing to the perception that drugs play more than a casual role in his life, a perception that Jack intentionally cultivated in the early years of his stardom and that has backfired on him.

He began talking publicly in 1970 about his use of drugs, for it was then that he was afforded a forum and that he appointed himself a representative of his "constituents." He felt that drugs such as marijuana should be legalized and that talking about using them might in some way contribute to the reform of laws prohibiting their use. "It's insane to have laws that are making criminals out of a huge percentage of the population," he said, "particularly when it's something that involves morality. I'm old-fashioned in that I don't want to see the entire world addicted to drugs—like the synthetic existence described in Brave New World—but I think it's an enormous leap from a little grass to that grim picture."[3] He often boasted of being in the vanguard of drug use. "I was one of the first people in the country to take acid [LSD]," he said, and "I was one of the first people in Hollywood out of the closet with marijuana."[4] He had written a film script about the use of LSD, The Trip, and had gone into great detail about using both marijuana and LSD while filming Easy Rider. From the way he emphasized that the director and cast had formed a pact not to use marijuana while filming *Carnal Knowledge*, one could infer that it's used routinely during all his work.

By 1972, the use of cocaine was becoming widespread in Hollywood and New York circles, and Jack said he had tried it but that it "didn't seem to do too much" for him. He also discussed reading Errol Flynn's autobiography, *My Wicked, Wicked Ways*, and of Flynn's use of cocaine as a sexual aid. "That's the real attraction of it," he said.[5]

One writer came to Jack's defense in the mid 1970s with an astonishing opinion. "Nicholson's reputation as a drug freak," he wrote, "has been overblown. He smokes cannabis, occasionally snorts cocaine, and has dropped a good deal of acid—at first under medical supervision, later mostly for kicks, no speed, no heroin."[6] By this time, Jack was describing his drug use as "moderate, under control," but there were rumors to the contrary, and also facts and circumstances that made his assessment questionable. He is said to have used "lots of cocaine, mostly at night" while filming *Goin' South* in 1978, which was cited as one of the reasons he was in no position to lecture John Belushi for using drugs.[7] He is reported to have kept two kinds of cocaine at his Mulholland Drive home, a downstairs sort for visitors and an upstairs kind for "special friends and women."[8] While Jack was not involved with any scandal regarding his own drug use, some of his close friends and acquaintances were.

Cathy Smith, the woman who pleaded guilty to involuntary manslaughter in John Belushi's death, was acquainted with Jack and even arranged a date for him with a model.[9] Then Roman Polanski, who directed Jack in *Chinatown*, and who was also a photographer, used Jack's house on Mulholland Drive for a photographic modeling session with a thirteen-year-old, whom he later was charged with drugging and raping. Jack was away at his place in Aspen at the time and was in no way implicated in the Polanski incident, but Anjelica was caught in the web. She was separating from Jack again at the time and happened to be at his house the day after the incident to get her belongings. The authorities arrived with a search warrant and in the process found a small amount of cocaine in her purse and arrested her. Anjelica had nothing to do with the Polanski incident, either, and the charges against her were subsequently dropped. Polanski ultimately jumped bail and fled to Europe before his trial date, where he remains.

In 1980, Jack was still talking to the entertainment press about drugs. "I still like to get high, I'd say about four times a week," he said, then added with a wink, "I think that's about average for an American." He also admitted that he didn't change his way of living even when his daughter, Jennifer (then a teenager), visited. "My daughter knows all the drugs I do," he said. "She's seen me do 'em."[10]

Finally, by 1981, he had decided that candor was getting him nowhere. After leading the charge for more than a decade, he noted that his one-man crusade was taking on the trappings of a carnival sideshow. "I don't feel obligated to go on with the case [for reforming narcotics laws]," he said. "I'm not feeling philanthropic enough to expose myself any longer. Where I used to feel that I was doing something for the general good, I now feel more like a kind of entertainment—what the weirdos are doing this week—and that's not really where I am, as anyone who really knows me is aware."[11]

A year later, he was even more reflective. "I'm sorry I ever said I smoked pot," he said. "If I'd known what happens to a public figure, I would have kept my mouth shut. I still don't like hiding what I do, especially if I don't think there's anything wrong with it, but it's twenty years later, now, and I feel I was stupid to have talked about it in the beginning. I probably didn't help people ease their feelings about it. The voting patterns about it haven't changed. And if I'd been more crafty, I wouldn't have done it. Because what I'm really interested in is my work, and it's trivializing to the work to have to approach it through this filter all the time."[12]

By 1984, he was reiterating his resolve not to speak publicly of his drug use. "I won't tell anybody anything like that ever again," he said.[13] But it was evident that stopping the flow of information served only to pique the public's interest. "I gave this press conference in Europe," he said, "and I said great stuff about . . . *Terms of Endearment,* and all they wrote about was cocaine, which I didn't even say *anything* about! They said stuff that they assumed because of my reputation. And I sued, because there you win [court] costs. I knew I wouldn't lose because what they said wasn't true."[14]

Jack spends a good deal of time in Europe, on vacations and

132

filming, as well as on promotion tours for the European releases of his films. The European press is aggressive and often quick to speculate obliquely about his alleged drug use, but there was one allegation that was not at all oblique. A British writer, reporting on his London interview with Jack in 1984, related how the interview ended with a smorgasbord of drugs. The interview took place in a London restaurant, where Jack and the interviewer were interrupted by a stranger, a man who was a fan of Jack's and who invited them to join him and his friend at their hotel "on an exploration into the hinterlands of ceremonial chemistry," which lasted the entire night. "The Main Attraction," wrote the interviewer, "was a large circular glass table on which were laid out, in the manner of a supper party, samples of every known stimulant known to man and even some that neither Jack nor I had ever come across before. . . . Some might have said, the perfect end to a perfect evening. . . . Much later, as we stood on the steps outside Blakes and watched the sun come up over the Roland Gardens, Jack replaced his jacket and dark glasses and grinned 'fit to bust.' 'You know, David [he said], we should do this more often' "[15]

It wasn't only aggressive journalists and critics who were speculating about Jack's drug use in the late 1970s and early 1980s. There were also whispers from Hollywood circles that even Jack's friends were genuinely alarmed about his use of drugs; this led a *Rolling Stone* magazine reporter to confront him in 1984 with specifics. She asked Jack to describe his drug use, and Jack replied, "Convivial." When asked what he meant by that, Jack said, "It means I have a good time. I don't drink, although the last couple years I've started to drink a little alcohol—a glass of wine, maybe two brandies at night after coffee." When asked whether he smoked marijuana, Jack said, "Why talk about it? I'm not helping anybody. I've no desire to conceal what I do, but I've tried not concealing it, and it has the opposite effect. People love to have a reason to level you. They don't have to deal with me as directly because they have this disqualifying clause in their perception of me. It's hard for me to think I live in a world where it's not good for you to be candid about something that, in your heart, there's nothing wrong with." The writer then asked whether Jack would be willing to say that he didn't use cocaine. "Would I say?" Jack said. "I really have decided I have nothing to say that's of any use to me or anyone

133

else." After this exchange, the writer got down to the concerns of Jack's intimates. "Some people," she said, "seem to be more worried about your health than your morals, in terms of your alleged drug use." To this Jack replied, "Doctor, cure yourself. I feel that most of the time I know what I'm doing. I missed no acting classes during the twelve years I was in class, and I haven't missed a day's work from illness in thirty years. I'll put my medical charts, my sanity charts up against anybody's. . . . As a workman, I'm known as a model of professionalism. I have to put up with being falsely described because it's unhip to bridle at it. Besides, it's just like womanizing. I'm not sure it ain't good for business."[16]

"I wanted to have a full stinger, because they'd never seen that in movies . . . but I couldn't get anything going because I knew everyone down there was waiting to see this thing."

Jack Nicholson[1]

By the time *Goin' South* was released in October 1978, Jack was busy at Elstree Studios in north London on *The Shining,* costarring Shelley Duvall and Benjamin "Scatman" Crothers, and directed by Stanley Kubrick. Based on a horror novel by Stephen King, *The Shining* is about a would-be writer who takes a job as caretaker of a mountain hotel that is closed for the winter. After being driven mad by the spirits who haunt the place, he tries to murder his wife and son. Though Jack's only other starring role in a feature-length horror film, *The Terror,* is now an embarrassment to him, there were a number of inducements that again attracted him to the genre as an actor. On a personal level, he has always taken an almost adolescent pleasure in fancying that he has a

16

ON THE EDGE

malevolent streak deep in the labyrinths of his personality, one that he could presumably explore and live through a film role. Even before the filming began, he was seriously savoring the prospect of truly affecting peoples' lives by causing them to have nightmares as a result of his portrayal.

There were professional inducements, as well. A horror film was a change of pace and in keeping with his desire to vary his roles, and he felt that the genre gave him license to move beyond what he considered the constraints of his naturalistic acting style. "When the material is as unusual as *The Shining*, dealing with ghosts and spirits," he said later, "the acting has to be larger than life. It's a demand of the material that's taken into account when designing the part. I play the character as a guy who's deeply pathological in the area of his marital relationships. . . . It's a demanding, highly difficult performance that's sort of balletic."[2] Finally, there was the inducement of working with the director, Stanley Kubrick, who admired Jack's work and with whom Jack wanted to work.

Kubrick had a reputation for mounting first-class productions. He was a perfectionist and a hard taskmaster, who sometimes worked his cast and crew to mental and physical exhaustion. He often worked within closed sets—presumably to preclude distractions and to keep his singular product under wraps until he was ready to present it to the public. He also took several times as long as most other directors to complete a film. So everyone connected with *The Shining* was prepared for a long and arduous shoot.

To ensure that Jack was comfortable for the duration, the production company rented a two-thousand-dollar-a-week house for him in fashionable Cheyne Walk on the Chelsea Embankment. It had four bedrooms and four baths and a garden with a sliding roof that could double as a dining area. It was reportedly in the garden, early in the shoot, that Jack took a "heavy fall" while trying to scale a low garden wall and injured his back so badly that he apparently missed several weeks' shooting.[3]

After his injury, Jack returned to work but continued sampling London's nightlife. He reportedly attended all the top parties, each with a different woman. "What nobody can understand," wrote one reporter, "is how he manages to keep up the pace. He has to be up at the crack of dawn . . . to drive to the studio—yet he is often the last to leave the party. The other night at 1 A.M. he was

still going strong, surrounded by a group of admiring females."⁴
Soon, however, Anjelica arrived to take up residence with him in
Cheyne Walk. Her presence put a damper on his "skunk"-chasing
escapades, and Stanley Kubrick's shooting schedule extinguished
the remaining fire. According to Anjelica, Jack would lurch into
the house at about 10:00 P.M., exhausted. They went out only
once, she said, and even then they were an hour and a half late
to meet Princess Margaret.

There was much talk of difficulties between Jack and Kubrick
on the set. One thing that particularly bothered Jack was that unlike other directors, who used stand-ins for the stars in the time-
consuming and always boring process of lighting the scenes to be
shot, Kubrick insisted that his stars stand in for themselves. Then,
too, there was his penchant for shooting the same scene time and
time again. Jack is said to have intervened on Scatman Crothers's
behalf when the director had the aging actor repeat a particularly
grueling scene until he was nearly exhausted. There were rumors
that Kubrick shot as many as a hundred takes of some scenes, rumors
that were always followed by denials from the production's publicist.
When the picture was completed, though, Crothers elaborated on
Kubrick's doing so many takes. "He had Jack Nicholson walk across
the street, no dialogue. Fifty takes," Crothers said. "He had Shelley,
Jack, and the kid [Danny Lloyd] walk across the street. Eighty-
seven takes, man. He always wants something new, and he doesn't
stop until he gets it."⁵

As usual, Jack came to the director's defense after the picture
wrapped. Though he admitted grumbling about having to be on
hand even as the sets were being lit, saying, "Just because you're
a perfectionist doesn't mean you're perfect," he defended the director's taking so long to shoot the film (ten months). "There are
always insane and preposterous legends about people who work in
movies and, because he's one of the outstanding people in his field,
his legends are even more preposterous than anyone else's. The
simple truth about Stanley is that he is the definition of how long
it actually takes to make a movie. I mean, everyone else is cutting
corners"⁶

Though *The Shining* was very popular with general audiences at
home and abroad and made a great deal of money, horror fans found
it unhorrifying, Stephen King fans thought it a travesty, and most

critics found it wanting. A few critics were pleased with the film and with Jack's performance, but the consensus was that Kubrick should have spent less time with the Steadicam and the technical aspect of the film and more time with the script, developing the characters so that their changes and actions were logically inevitable—and therefore horrifying—as they were in the novel. As it turned out, the film fell short of Kubrick's stated desire to make "the best horror movie ever," a movie that had to be, in Kubrick's words, "plausible, use no cheap tricks, have no holes in the plot and no failure in motivation. It must be a scary horror story without insulting the intelligence of the audience."[7] The *New Yorker* critic Pauline Kael said, "The film is about tracking. . . . Kubrick loves the ultra-smooth tracking shots made possible by the Steadicam." And critic Henry Bromwell wrote, "Kubrick simply makes Jack an exaggerated, highly stylized boogeyman rising from the shadows to frighten children."[8]

After a little rest and relaxation from the rigors of working with Kubrick, Jack again teamed up with his friend Bob Rafelson to do *The Postman Always Rings Twice*, a remake of the Tay Garnett–directed 1946 adaptation of the 1934 James M. Cain novel that had starred Lana Turner and John Garfield. Jack's interest in the project dated back to 1972, when he committed to do an MGM version of it with Michelle Phillips, *The Three-cornered Circle*, which was never produced. He presumably got Paramount Pictures to buy the remake rights and took the project to Rafelson.

Jack's primary interest in doing a remake of the film was owing to its sexuality; the story is so inherently lusty—not a love story, but one of obsessive lust—that only a sanitized version could be adapted for the silver screen of the 1940s. He said he did *Postman* because he hadn't done a film about sex and hadn't had much opportunity to do what he called "sexual acting," which he felt he had always done well in acting classes.

Postman is a Depression-era tale of a masochistic drifter who finds a job at a gas station/café owned by a middle-aged man and his young wife. The wife and the drifter are so overcome with lust for each other that they kill the husband and get away with his murder. Their lustful tale ends when the wife is killed in an automobile accident.

Jack and Rafelson were both intrigued with the idea of bringing a *sexually* faithful adaptation of the story to the screen (they decided against using the ironic and moralistic ending whereby the drifter, having gotten away with murdering Cora's husband, was wrongly charged with murdering her), and screenwriter David Mamet wrote a script that was exactly what they wanted. Their next concern was finding an actress suitable for the part of Cora, the young wife. "What I like about Cain," Jack said, "is that his women are very strong. Villainesses. You think of Joan Crawford or Bette Davis in those roles. . . ." Meryl Streep was approached to play the feminine lead, but she was pregnant and so the part went to Jessica Lange, whom Jack had tested for *Goin' South.*

Rafelson said he shot the film as though for an X rating, but cut it for an R rating. There was one shot Jack wanted that Rafelson probably would have had to cut around, but it was never filmed. In talking about the absence of nudity and other stylistic choices reflected in the film, Jack said, "I also liked the idea of an obvious, fresher image. There was a shot I wanted to do when he first makes love to her, when he backs her off the chopping block [in the kitchen]—a reverse angle with my clothes on, but I wanted to have a full stinger, because they'd never seen that in movies. I just knew this odd image would be a stunner. Well, I went upstairs and worked on it for forty-five minutes, but I couldn't get anything going because I knew everyone was waiting down there to see this thing. Somebody else might have said I was a pervert, but in my terms this would have been extremely artful."

Postman was a critical and financial failure at home, but it was well received abroad; Jack noted, however, that it outgrossed even the hugely successful *Chinatown* in every foreign market except Venezuela. "Of course, the movie was better released foreign than it was here," he said. "Here it was poorly done." Most American critics faulted the directing as too leisurely and controlled, and a few said it lacked the tension even of the 1946 version. It was thought too protracted, and objective almost to the point of abstraction, which, ironically, is in a sense what the screenwriter, director, and star were striving for. They may have been too successful—too cerebral in their handling of the material. Jack was disappointed with the film's poor reception in the United States, but he wasn't surprised. He later lamented that American audiences like sexy films, not sexual ones, and there was nothing sexy about

139

a story of lust with sadomasochistic overtones. Ultimately, *Postman* is one of those films that when judged in the body of Jack's work will probably be viewed with more esteem than it was in its day.

As he had done with *Tommy* and *The Last Tycoon* in the mid-1970s, Jack committed to a supporting role in his next film, *Reds*, which was released in 1981. It was produced and directed by his friend Warren Beatty, who also cowrote the script and starred in the film with his real-life lover of the day, Diane Keaton. With the Russian Revolution as backdrop, *Reds* is the true love story of American journalists John Reed and Louise Bryant. Reed, a socialist and political activist, witnessed the Russian Revolution and is the only American buried in the Kremlin wall.

Jack is known to be deliberate in considering material and cautious in making commitments, but he made an exception for *Reds*; he hadn't even read the complete script when he agreed to do the film. "I was in it so early that all I heard was Warren's concept of it," he said. "I like to think that by being there early, and being genuinely excited about the project, I provided a good lead-off for him."[9]

Beatty needed moral support. It had taken him several years to put the project together—and for good reason. Even though he was a proven money-maker as both an actor and a producer—he had coproduced two very successful films that he also had starred in (*Bonnie and Clyde* and *Heaven Can Wait*)—he had never directed one alone (he codirected *Heaven Can Wait*). That fact was enough to send studio executives scrambling for tranquilizers had he proposed to direct even a small film with a modest budget of $4 or $5 million. What he proposed instead was for the studio to put up seven times that amount—$35 million—so that he could give directing a try. What he had in mind was a respectful film about an American Communist, at a time when anti-Communism seemed the country's only political driving force, a force that helped sweep another actor, Ronald Reagan, into the Oval Office. It was a seemingly unimaginable project, but the studio moguls agreed to back it, presumably with the provision that they would have script approval and that Beatty would star in it.

The nature of the subject alone made getting approval of the shooting script exacting. Beatty needed a writer who was not only an excellent craftsman but who also had a feeling for the subtle complexities of turn-of-the-century politics. For this, he chose a socialist British playwright, Trevor Griffiths, to write the screenplay. The studio judged Griffiths's first script "too political," and so Beatty and the playwright spent three months at London's Dorchester Hotel rewriting it. The rewrite was also found unacceptable, and Griffiths is reported to have abandoned the project. Robert Towne and Elaine May were then brought in as script doctors (without screen credit), and they eventually refashioned the script in a manner that Beatty found acceptable and that met with the studio's approval.

Jack portrayed playwright Eugene O'Neill in the film. In preparation for the role, he studied biographies of the playwright and discovered a kindred spirit. "I did a tremendous amount of research," he said. "It was intoxicating. I must have read a thousand pages about the guy. His relationships with women were fabulous. I mean, he went through kind of an arc that I can identify with. He was like most Irishmen—mad about tempestuous women, women who sort of keep his socks in the sink. But until he got someone who more or less eliminated the romance and just sort of managed him, he didn't start to do this tremendous amount of work. . . . I like his philosophy, which is sort of shown in *Reds*— that if you're an artist, it's art over politics, over sociology, over everything."[10] "Jack later said that it would have been "criminal" had he not been good in the role. "I had everything going for me—a very stimulating actress [Keaton] to work with in most scenes, a director who is fond of my work and who knows what he likes about it, and a part that is beautifully written. I feel silly getting credit for it. . . . Every once in a while a part comes along where you can say, 'I think I can do this better than anyone else.' I think that was true of *Reds*."[11]

Jack so identified with the playwright that he fell in love with Diane Keaton during the filming. In life, the woman Keaton portrayed, Louise Bryant, was in love with the romantic idealist John Reed, the part played by Beatty. At the same time, Bryant was drawn to—and had an affair with—Eugene O'Neill. When Jack was later asked whether he had developed a crush on Keaton, he said, "I don't want to hide behind this, but during the production that's the way it began to feel . . . my character was attracted to Keaton's character. And I'm focused on my job all the time. In

141

fact, during the work, I would allow myself to get over-inflamed about it with Warren right there—just to see what would happen. Absolutely nothing happened between Diane and me."¹² Jack's interest in Keaton was apparently so obvious during the shooting that the show-business media took note and exploited it, hinting at an affair. Jack and Beatty had been attracted to the same woman on occasion—at different times—but no one who knew of the basic honesty and respect that characterized their long friendship doubted that while Jack's interest in Keaton during the filming was genuine, his friendship with her was platonic.

The reviews of *Reds* were mixed, but almost all were respectful. A few expressed the wish that Beatty had spent less time on the love story and more on the revolution—one review was bannered A MAN, A WOMAN AND, OH, YES, A REVOLUTION—but, in fact, *Reds* was a relatively accurate account of the times, and of necessity the politics had to be simplified and subordinate to the love story. Beatty won an Oscar for Best Director, as did Maureen Stapleton for her supporting role. Jack was nominated as Best Supporting Actor but didn't win. He was very happy with his performance, though, as were most critics. Pauline Kael, the *New Yorker* critic, who had lost patience with his acting in recent work, liked him in *Reds*. "The jitters and freak exhilaration of Nicholson's recent performances are gone," she wrote. "He isn't just throwing off sparks here . . . he sinks down into himself and plays a quiet, deeply bitter man."¹³

142   A dividend that Jack found gratifying was a letter he received from O'Neill's daughter, Oona, whom O'Neill never spoke to after she married Charlie Chaplin. After seeing Jack's portrayal of O'Neill, Oona wrote to thank Jack for reawakening feelings for her father again. "The greatest compliment I ever got," Jack said.

Jack had nothing planned after *Reds*. He had been winding down his schedule in order to take a long vacation when he was suddenly offered an opportunity to work with English director Tony Richardson, whom he admired. He had met Richardson in Paris while trying to peddle *The Shooting* and *Ride in the Whirlwind* in 1966.

Richardson was in preproduction on *The Border*, an action-adventure film that he was doing for Universal Pictures, when for some reason the starring role was vacated. With the unaccustomed luxury of unstructured time before him, Jack agreed to do the film.

"We always planned to work together some day," he said, "and when this came up—I think someone else had dropped out—the timing was right. I'd been wanting to do an action picture for some time. After all, I soon won't be young enough to do them anymore. That, coupled with the fact that *The Border* had a pertinent social theme, attracted me."[14]

The Border is the story of Charlie Smith, a decent and hardworking Immigration Services investigator who transfers to the border patrol and is assigned duty as an officer on the Texas-Mexican border. What he really had wanted was the life of a forest ranger, but he took the border-patrol job to placate his wife (Valerie Perrine), who is the kind who lies around the house eating bonbons and whose idea of the good life is a condo in El Paso and an open charge account in every store in town.

What Charlie finds on the border are baby snatchers, who make a living selling infants; smugglers, who run aliens across the border for profit; and border-patrol officers who have grown inhumane, cynical, and corrupt in their impossible efforts to stop the flow of illegal aliens across the border. Charlie, too, is corrupted until he finds cause to rise above temptation.

When the studio executives viewed the initial rough cut of the film, they didn't like what they saw and ordered extensive changes; the film was too violent and depressing, reportedly ending with Jack's character wrecking the boarder-patrol station after discovering that his coworkers were not only corrupt but murderers as well. A new upbeat ending was shot, wherein Jack's character saves a widowed young Mexican mother and her children. Several violent scenes were cut, together with two sex scenes that Jack had objected to early in the shooting because he felt them too reminiscent of scenes in *Postman*. "An actor doesn't want to burden his director with his past career," Jack said, "but I felt the scenes shouldn't be in and I said so."[15]

The studio was ultimately satisfied with the changes, but one writer, David Ehrenstein, felt that by trying to turn Jack into "a slightly scruffy Gary Cooper" in the editing room, the filmmakers went against the grain of his screen persona and fragmented the story line in the process.

Jack's back had troubled him during the shooting, perhaps owing to his injury from the fall he had taken in London when he was

143

doing *The Shining*. There were times when he couldn't sit, and had to lie down in the backseat of the vehicles that transported him. Working with a troublesome injury and redoing the film's ending made the shoot longer and more arduous than he had anticipated, so when *The Border* wrapped, he was more eager than ever for the vacation he had planned. He spent the summer of 1980 in Europe with Sam Spiegel, aboard his yacht. "Just like his sidekick," Jack said. "He was certainly an inspiration; those movies he made in the fifties *were* the movies, just about. Sam's lesson to me was always go for quality."[16] Then having recuperated, he spent the winter alone—except for his cook—at his place in Aspen, skiing.

When he finally came out of the mountains to promote *The Border* in mid-January 1982, he did so reluctantly. He wasn't mentally prepared to go back to work, had apparently not yet resolved the crisis in confidence that had gripped him in the wake of a string of films that had met with critical hostility and fan indifference. Hitting the road to thump the drum for an action melodrama that had just been released from intensive care in the cutting room was not a joyous prospect. However, to his surprise—and presumably to his great relief—he discovered that during his year off he had become hot again, not only with his fans but also with those of his critics who had been leveling broadsides at him for the past three years.

144

> "That phase of my work is all behind me. The responses to it, the mis-responses to it. . . . Fresh deck."
>
> *Jack Nicholson*[1]

I've done a terrible piece of timing," Jack said. "I'm not ready to stop skiing, and here I am, hot."[2] It was the first week in February 1982. He had just arrived in New York City for his promotion tour and was surprised to find that movie-industry tastemakers had rediscovered him while he was away. His popularity had risen with his nomination for an Oscar as Best Supporting Actor in *Reds* and with early critical praise for his performance in *The Border*. The film would ultimately play to mixed reviews, but nearly all the critics were pleased with Jack's performance and applauded him for being "back in form" again; their reviews made it clear that they liked his acting the way it was and wished that he would stop trying to change it. Jack was ambivalent about this turn of events: happy to be liked again but disappointed and angry that his "constituents" and

17
BREAKING HARD

critics were not more patient with him, would not let him break free from the chains of his naturalistic acting style. Indeed, while he had seen himself as soaring free for his art, the reviews suggested that many critics had looked upon his quest as that of a lunatic Prometheus, hurling himself at the moon, which he has mistaken as the source of fire.

In reflecting on the films Jack had done since winning the Oscar for *Cuckoo's Nest,* writer Jamie Wolf said it was apparent that he had "thought hard and seriously" about his screen persona and acting style and about what he considered to be the dreadful temptation to rely on something that works (his screen persona) and that therefore will have a sameness about it. "Once you're a known entity," Jack said, "and not only you but other people know what can succeed about you, this is the beginning of disaster. Believe me, you're in some kind of declining creative vitality when they start writing to suit what they imagine your talent is—when your job is always to stretch that."[3] While there's truth to this view, it doesn't apply to Jack and never has. Some were saying that he was becoming easily bored with acting, that he didn't enjoy it as he once had. Wolf noted that Jack "made a specific craft decision involving aspects of challenge and risk," whether owing to creative restlessness or to a genuine (if unfounded) fear of losing the magic, of becoming known. Rather than continue to stretch by changing his familiar persona with subtle variations to effect the difference he sought—which he had always done well and successfully and which, Wolf notes, is a "long and respectable tradition of American movie-star acting that includes Fonda and Tracy and Stewart and Cagney"—Jack went to the extreme of experimenting with radical departures, which Wolf called a "series of strange eye-rolling, eyebrow-darting, broadly melodramatic performances that seemed willfully eccentric and larger than life."

The paradox, Wolf suggests, is that the technique of using subtle variations, which Nicholson abandoned for a while, was producing the effect he sought, while his radical departures—his attempts at being bigger by playing more broadly—have the sameness about them that he was trying to avoid.

When Jack was asked why he thought the critics were saying that *The Border* showed a return to previous work, he said, "Probably because I was able to give a naturalistic performance in that film.

And that wasn't possible in the films that preceded it. *Goin' South* was a farce; *The Shining* was a Grand Guignol; *Postman* was a film noir; *Reds* was biographical. All had their own stylistic demands. This one didn't, and in many ways it was easier to do."⁴ Whatever the reason for his radical departure in style, the realization that most critics and fans weren't buying it wasn't wasted on him. "That phase of my work is all behind me," he said. "The responses to it, the misresponses to it. . . . Fresh deck."

Jack committed to his next film on the telephone. The role was a supporting one, and he didn't know the director, James L. Brooks. He didn't even ask whether Brooks had ever directed a movie (he hadn't). "I made the deal with him based on the fact that he wrote a brilliant script and the way he talked to me on the telephone," Jack said. "By now I can tell if someone is talented. And he's an easy call."⁵

Brooks was a writer, director, and producer of several very successful television series,⁶ and the film was *Terms of Endearment*, a comedy-drama based on Larry McMurtry's novel about a mother-daughter relationship spanning three decades. Brooks cast Shirley MacLaine (as the prim widowed mother, Aurora Greenway) and Debra Winger in the leads, with the men in their lives—Jeff Daniels, Jack, John Lithgow, and Danny DeVito—as supporting players. Jack's character was the only one created expressly for the film. Aurora has many suitors in the novel, but in order to add measures of romantic comedy to counterpoint the film's subsequent somber tones, Brooks consolidated the suitors in the person of Aurora's next-door neighbor, middle-aged playboy Garrett Breedlove, a paunchy former astronaut who has found heaven on earth chasing young women and fast times and with whom Aurora has an affair. It was a part that could have been written for Jack, but it wasn't. Paul Newman, among others, is said to have turned it down. "That was always the uncastable part," Brooks said. "The man had to be over forty, and there's no undiscovered actor over forty whom I could imagine doing this part. It had to be a star. The problem is that there are two roles in the picture that are bigger than his, and so how are you going to get a star to play him?"⁷

Jack didn't have to be persuaded. The role was the kind of challenge he liked. "I'm in my forties," he said at the time, "and if I'm going to continue to grow as a person and an artist, I can't keep playing thirty-five-year-old ideas of romance." He was so sure of the project that he predicted an Oscar for himself and for the film even before the shoot started.

Terms was very successful at the box office, and did even better with the Academy of Motion Picture Arts and Sciences than Jack predicted. It was named Best Picture; Shirley MacLaine won an Oscar as Best Actress; Brooks won two, one for his directing and one for his screenplay adaptation; and Jack was named Best Supporting Actor, an award he had been after since *Easy Rider* and one that made him a member of a very select trio. Only Jack Lemmon and Robert De Niro had received Oscars in both Best Actor and Best Supporting Actor categories before him.

Several months before Jack won his Oscar for *Terms*, a writer asked him why a superstar like him had chosen to do supporting roles in two of his most recent films. Jack took offense at the roles being called supporting ones; he said that he preferred to think of them as short parts that would not be as singularly effective if another actor played them. As to his choosing short parts, he said, "Well, if I read a part that makes me carry the movie, I'd feel like I was in trouble playing it." After a moment's reflection, he added, "You've got to have a few worries in your mind."[8] He was considering his options at the time and had yet to be approached for the lead in his next picture, *Prizzi's Honor*, but if any project had caused him a few worries, it was that one.

He didn't think *Prizzi's Honor* was his kind of material, and he didn't understand the lead character. He would not have given the part a second thought under other circumstances. Both Anjelica and her father, director John Huston, were committed to the project, however, and it was largely in deference to them that he agreed to do it. He could do worse than put his trust in a director like John Huston, and the film meant a great deal to Anjelica. It was her first substantial role in a major motion picture, and of all people, Jack knew what a pivotal role in a big picture could do for a career. Anjelica had been working hard for such a break.

In 1980, six years after she gave up a modeling career and then did little else other than live Jack's life, Anjelica was thrown through the windshield of her automobile in a head-on collision with another vehicle. She was twenty-eight at the time, and in the horrifying moment of the collision she thought, It's all over, and it hasn't even begun.[9]

Her physical injuries were relatively minor ones—her nose was broken in four places—but the psychic disturbances were not. She suddenly saw the striking parallel between her mother's death and her own brush with death and between her mother's life and her own. It caused her to reflect on where and who she was. She made subtle adjustments to her private life. She maintained her relationship with Jack but moved from the Mulholland Drive house to a small rental a few minutes' drive away. She continued to frequent Jack's place to have dinner with him and often to stay over, but in her own home she learned to live with and for herself again. She also decided to become serious about acting. Her mother had been a Balanchine dancer; her father was a very talented artist, writer, actor, and director, and she had playacted since she was old enough to talk. She came by her talent naturally, and she determined to develop it. She took acting classes from Peggy Feury, a well-known West Coast instructor, and she began doing small parts in plays, television series, and movies. She portrayed an animal trainer in *Postman*, did bits in television, including two episodes of "Laverne and Shirley," a popular program of the day. She starred as Emily in a short HBO film for television, an adaptation of William Faulkner's short story "A Rose for Emily"; she appeared in a modestly produced play in Los Angeles; and she did small roles in low-budget genre films, including the part of a fearsome swordswoman in *Ice Pirates*.

149

When producer John Foreman signed John Huston to direct *Prizzi's Honor*, he screened *Ice Pirates* and agreed with the director that Anjelica would be well cast in the role of Maerose Prizzi, the granddaughter of a Brooklyn, New York, Mafia don. In the story, Maerose is still in love with her former fiancé, Charley Partanna, a cunning but slow-witted and humorless Prizzi-family hit man, and throughout the story she plays out her scheme to get him back, knowing that he must be allowed to run free before he'll ever come to the realization of what's good for him—her.

Once Anjelica was set for the part, she is said to have broached the subject with Jack of playing Charley Partanna. Jack read the script and then the novel and decided he didn't want to do the picture. Though *Prizzi's Honor* was represented to him as a satire or black comedy, he didn't see anything satirical or funny about a story in which a hit man kills people and even slits his own wife's throat. Even so, Anjelica finally convinced him—presumably with John Huston's help—that the role would be different from anything he had done, and a challenge. Jack wanted to work with John Huston and with Anjelica, and though working in a movie and a role he didn't understand was not the kind of challenge he was looking for, he more or less suppressed his better instincts and plunged ahead.

Jack always searches for positive aspects in the characters he portrays, especially if the character is a largely unsavory one, but he had to stretch in a convoluted manner to get a grip on Charley Partanna. "I put my not understanding the material together with the character's dumbness into a kind of dynamic on how to play him," Jack said.[10] It was the sort of departure from persona that he would have relished had he liked the story and understood the character. But the most courageous part of his decision was not in burying his persona, which he had often done in his performances, but in taking on a role that he didn't understand.

It took perhaps even more courage to do what Anjelica did. She had to work through layers of fear—not only the fear that attends a relative newcomer's tackling such a complex role but also the fear of working with her father again after sixteen years and the fear of disappointing him again as she thought she had in *A Walk with Love and Death*. So both she and Jack were apprehensive about the film.

They stayed at separate Manhattan hotels throughout the Brooklyn shoot. Jack stayed at his favorite, the Carlyle; Anjelica wouldn't stay there this time because Jack was beginning to live his role, as he usually does when he's getting into character. "There were elements of the hit man in Jack at the time," Anjelica said, "and I didn't want to be around him too much."[11] Even so, they met for hours to talk about their roles, and Jack helped her with technique.

While Anjelica worked on motivation with her acting coach, Jack took to the Brooklyn streets. He patronized the bars and cafés, studying the accents and gestures of the locals. It seemed to him that Italian-American men didn't move their upper lip much when they spoke, so he did the film with tissue stuffed between his gum and upper lip to immobilize it. He also ate a lot of pasta, which he loves, and tried for what he called the "two-ton Tony Galento" walk, with palms facing backward.

John Huston's direction made it a pleasant filming. He gave the actors wide latitude and gentle guidance. "He let us go as we should all let our pets go,"[12] Jack said. His method of shooting scenes made Jack's job more difficult, though. It often takes Jack a couple of weeks to sink into character. One method he uses to explore facets of the character he's portraying is to take advantage of the director's own explorations—the reshooting of scenes from different angles and attitudes. This would have been particularly useful to Jack in trying to fathom a character such as Charley Partanna. Huston, however, was one of those directors who camera-cut, who did much of his editing in his head rather than in the cutting room; he often envisioned exactly what he wanted in a scene and shot from one angle and in one take, if possible, or with as few takes as necessary to get what he expected from his actors. Jack isn't comfortable with camera-cutting, as either an actor or director. "If you only do one take, you don't really know what you did," he said. "You don't get to refine it. You come home and think of the thirty-five things you might've thrown in the stew."[13]

The film played to large audiences and to mostly good reviews. There were critics who didn't appreciate the humor in it, while others thought it very funny. Some didn't like Jack in the role and felt that his intelligence detracted from the portrayal, felt that he was obviously playing dumb rather then being dumb. However, most people liked his performance. Richard Schickel of *Time* thought it one of his boldest, and felt that Huston had found in Jack an actor who matched his own subtlety and nerve. Pauline Kael of *The New Yorker* was impressed by the film's "daring comic tone," calling it *"The Godfather* acted out by the Munsters," and taking particular delight in the "blurred expressions" Jack used to reflect Charley Partanna's dumbness, while David Ansen of *Newsweek* noted how Jack's "whole face comes back into focus" in Charley's rare moments of comprehension.

Though his performance had a few detractors, it was clear that for most people Jack had risen to the challenge, and quite brilliantly. The critical notices must have pleased him, but his attention was fixed on Anjelica's performance. "Isn't she terrific?" he said after

151

the film's premiere. "There's nothing in that character she didn't get. She's done something great, really great!" Members of the Academy agreed. She was awarded an Oscar as Best Supporting Actress for her performance, and John Huston, who in 1948 had directed his father, Walter, in an Academy Award performance in *The Treasure of the Sierra Madre,* became the only director ever to have guided both a parent and an offspring in Oscar-winning performances.

Following *Prizzi's Honor,* Jack was set to star in *The Two Jakes,* a sequel to *Chinatown,* but the project collapsed just three days before shooting was to begin, so he happened to be free when he was offered a role in another picture that was also in trouble. The film was *Heartburn,* written by Nora Ephron and based on her novel about a woman (Rachel) whose marriage is wrecked by a philandering husband (Mark) who cheats on her during her pregnancies. This is alleged to be a thinly disguised account of her own marriage breakup with Carl Bernstein, the Washington *Post* journalist of Watergate fame. It's said that Bernstein had not liked his ex-wife's portrayal of him in the novel, and fearing that the movie would cast him in the same light, he demanded and got script approval. Mandy Patinkin had been set to play the Bernstein character, Mark Forman, but he left the production when he saw that, owing to script changes, about all that remained of the character he had signed to play was the name. That's when a call went out to Jack.

Three days after he read the script, he was at work on the film. He claims he didn't know his character's name when they shot the first scene. It was not the kind of film he would ordinarily have signed for, and he says he probably shouldn't have considered it. He did, however, and for three reasons. The director was Mike Nichols, with whom he had done *Carnal Knowledge* and *The Fortune.* His costar was Meryl Streep, who was playing the Nora Ephron part (as Rachel) and whom Jack greatly admired and had wanted to work with in *Postman.* The third reason was another of the negatives that seem to challenge him—such as his use of "not understanding the material" to play Charley Partanna. "I'd never been hired specifically to *not* play someone," he said of taking the role in *Heartburn.* "And I was hired to not play Carl. I liked that idea; it's a provocative idea for an actor."[14]

It was coincidental that both Jack and Mike Nichols knew Carl

Bernstein. The journalist had even invited Nichols to lunch when he learned that he would be directing the film. Nichols reportedly told Bernstein that the film would be made no matter who directed it and that he would be better off with a friend at the helm. Besides reading widely in politics and current affairs, Jack has been involved with political campaigns. He actively had supported Robert Kennedy and California Governor Jerry Brown; he had attended the Democratic National Convention in support of former Senator George McGovern when he was a Presidential candidate. He also had campaigned for former Senator Gary Hart in his Presidential bid, pouring over Hart's position papers in order to represent him better. He had met with Bernstein a couple of times at political functions, and so knew the person he was not portraying.

"Mark was written as a sort of uninteresting cad," Jack said, "and we wanted a likable character, see. And so I said, 'Fine. Let me play the part backwards. Don't rewrite anything for me; I know where the problems are, and let me see if I can't do it with what I do.' Which is act. If you play characters for charm, it's most often cloying, so here was an opportunity where you *had* to bring a little bit of that quality. You get within that framework and you're doing things that you might feel a little bit showboaty doing in another kind of character. It was fun to do."[15]

What made the shoot even more enjoyable for Jack was Meryl Streep. "She's my idol," he said. "That rapport was great and almost instant. Like my first tough scene. I sort of blew it when I did it; it's the scene around the fountain kind of later [when Mark goes to New York to coax Rachel home]. But Meryl was so good in it. I mean it's a very different feeling when you're acting and someone else is carrying you, and that's definitely true in that scene. I was all at sea; I was floundering around, but I could see that we would be fine because she was doing great."[16]

Heartburn opened in July of 1986. It was a well-made, well-acted film with good moments, but the fact that it was fashioned by some of the brightest stars in the business and based upon a best-selling novel didn't help it at the box office. The general consensus among critics was that it was a handsome presentation but a hollow one. Many suggested that changing the male lead's character took away the abrasive edge that the story needed.

Jack was preparing for his next film while he promoted *Heartburn*.

153

"I've been studying to play the Devil," he said. Then, with what was described as a "demonic grin," he added, "Of course, a lot of people think I've been preparing for it all my life."[17] The film was *The Witches of Eastwick,* a humorous battle-of-the-sexes fantasy that, critic David Denby suggested, could be likened to Fellini's eye view of Jack Nicholson romping at home with friends. Based very loosely on John Updike's novel, it's the story of three New England women who are dissatisfied with men who can't relate naturally to liberated women; they share with each other their fantasies of finding a man who can. Having had too much wine one night, the women, played by Susan Sarandon, Cher, and Michelle Pfeiffer, half-jokingly perform an invocation, and are later stunned to find they've summoned a satanic visitor in the person of Darryl Van Horne (Jack), who is certainly at ease with his masculinity and with females, and who proclaims himself "just your average horny little devil." Though charming and funny, Darryl is also unkempt and slightly smelly and more than a bit too earthy for their taste. Nevertheless, he seduces each of them, and they're dazzled and delighted until they realize that he has reduced their liberated state to the degree that, as a male, he has power over them. This, it's suggested, is a condition they want and also don't want at the same time. They don't want it more than they want it, however, so they initiate a rite to divest him of his power and send him back from whence he came. Darryl is bewildered when he realizes that they are destroying him because he is the embodiment of their fulfilled wishes. Even as he is being destroyed, he lurches into a church and rails at the heavens: "Women—a mistake, or did He do it to us on purpose?"

To prepare for the role, Jack took violin lessons to learn how to hold the instrument properly. Though one of his two dogs found his violin playing entertaining, the same cannot be said for others in his household. Jack also read widely for the role. "I've read a lot of huge, studious books that deal with the Dark Ages," he said. "One of the things I came across is the big, long—seems like a century-long—debate about the definition of God. And the only thing they could come up with is that anything definite you can say about God must be supported by its paradoxical opposite. And that's what life is all about, this paradoxical situation."[18] He was said to have had "high ambitions" for his performance. "When I played *Carnal Knowledge,*" he said, "I knew that women weren't going to like me for a while. That was a given. I'm going to play the Devil. And I don't want to play him safely. I want people to think that Jack Nicholson *is* the Devil. I want them to be worried."[19]

What finally appeared on screen is at variance with the kind of film Jack suggested he was preparing for. It's also different in tone from the approach director George Miller had in mind. Miller's concept of the Devil was not as the stereotypical figure of evil incarnate but as a natural man. "My Devil had to be a Pan," he said, ". . . moving from community to community, causing all women to abandon themselves sexually to him, and so enraging the menfolk—this despite the fact that he is not conventionally handsome. The men can't understand why the women do it, and neither for that matter can the women. But his total self-confidence is what allows him to enjoy their favors, impregnate all the women, then move on. To a degree, Christian concepts of chastity for women were created by a male-dominated society to protect themselves from such a presence."[20]

Until a friend persuaded him to reconsider, Miller didn't want to cast Jack in the role. "My first instinct was: In getting someone for the Devil, you need an actor who is totally unlike the Devil, and Jack clearly has an impish quality. . . . Then, I realized he is like a two-hundred-year-old child: very wise in many ways—even beyond his years—but with a certain innocence and naiveté we expect from someone younger. The moment I saw that, I knew he was the only actor to bring a humanity to the role, to pull the Devil out of stereotype."[21]

The approach to telling the story that the director had initially taken and for which Jack had prepared was shot but was left in the cutting room with a number of other approaches. Indeed, according to Miller, there were, in effect, eight versions to chose from. Even as the cameras rolled, the producers made changes, unable to decide what form they wanted their film to take. They drove the director, the screenwriter, Michael Cristofer and the actors to distraction. Throughout the shoot, Cher and Michelle Pfeiffer—who had campaigned for a role in the film just to work with Jack—talked about walking off the picture. Owing to the inadequate wardrobe they were furnished for their roles, the women were angry with the producers, anyway; and then when the producers began changing the movie they had signed to do, they became incensed. They even

155

performed a rite, half-jokingly, to give the producers a venereal disease.

Finally, in an effort to keep the film rolling and to placate the producers, the director decided to do eight takes of each scene, beginning with a subdued naturalistic approach on the first take, then playing the scene more broadly with each successive take. "That allowed us to decide later in the editing room, what kind of tone we would have for the film," Miller said. "The movie you see is made up almost exclusively of the eighth takes. Simply, we sensed in retrospect that the broader takes were the ones that played best."[22]

The film did well at the box office but played to mixed reviews. Some critics, like *The New Yorker*'s Pauline Kael, generally liked Jack in the role: "Jack Nicholson entertains himself in *Witches,*" she said, "and damned if he doesn't entertain us, too." But some, like David Ansen of *Newsweek*, felt Jack was again too near the edge of self-parody. Jack had said he wanted audiences to think he was the Devil, wanted them to worry, but as Ansen points out, "How can an audience be surprised and alarmed by Horne, when we're so instantly indulgent of Nicholson?"[23] Again, it was the broader acting style that allowed the Nicholson persona to show through, that traded on known qualities, that seemed the same. Many noted the obvious similarities between Jack's portrayals in *The Shining* and *Witches,* and a few critics faulted him again for going over the top and into the stratosphere. Judging from the comments he made while preparing for the role, however, he would rather have put a sinister spin on the Devil's tale with a frightening, naturalistic performance—indeed, he had intended to do so. Along with the director, he deferred to the producer's wishes, though. As usual, he closed ranks with the production team to honor his professional credo: Save the film.

One of the powers that usually devolve to superstars is the influence their interest can exert, particularly in bringing projects to the screen. It's a power that has eluded Jack with frustrating frequency. Even after *Terms of Endearment*, when he was armed with two Oscars and a large box-office following, Jack saw two film projects in which he had expressed interest collapse for want of financial backing. He takes such rejections in stride professionally, but he can't help feeling personally offended by them as reflections of the industry's lack of confidence in his choice of material. For this reason alone, he must have been gratified when producer Keith Barish initiated production of *Ironweed* largely owing to Jack's interest in playing the lead. There were also other aspects about the film that he found gratifying. It offered a challenging part for him to play in a powerful story well told, and there was also a fine part in it for Meryl Streep, whose interest in it he had stirred as a vehicle for their reunion.

Brazilian director Hector Babenco was on vacation when he read William Kennedy's Pulitzer Prize–winning novel, *Ironweed*. He was haunted by the characters and the story, and he became obsessed with the desire to direct it for the screen—so obsessed that he continued to pursue the matter even after he discovered that the screen rights belonged to a producer who refused to consider him as director and who even refused to put him in touch with William Kennedy. Babenco eventually traced Kennedy to his home in Albany, New York, and went there for a weekend visit; he stayed nearly two months. Apparently convinced that the producer who owned the movie rights could not get the project started, Babenco and Kennedy decided to invest their time and talent purely on speculation. With Babenco's suggestions and encouragement, Kennedy wrote the screenplay that eventually was sent to Jack. With Jack's interest, producer Keith Barish purchased the film rights from the other producer and began production.

Ironweed is about 1930s street people. It takes place in Albany, New York, during the dead of winter, and concerns an alcoholic drifter, Francis Phelan (Jack), who returns to Albany—he had abandoned his wife and two children there twenty years earlier—where, living in the streets, he sees the symbols of a past that haunts him. He again faces the furies that drove him on his aimless and drunken wanderings. With him is his companion of nine years, Helen (Streep), a mentally troubled former concert pianist who is helpless on the streets and whom Francis tries to look after as best he can in his alcoholic fashion. It is, in director Babenco's words, a story of "wandering characters without destinies," and the story was particularly poignant for him because he identifies with the wanderers—a comparison that could apply to Jack, as well. "Who am I?" Babenco said. "I am a walker, someone who is wondering about the meaning of life, trying to put together his inner questions with his work. I cannot separate the man and the profession."[24]

The shoot began in winter on location in Albany during bad snowstorms. There was almost fifteen inches of snow on the ground and Babenco had to shoot around the weather. He had to start with the interiors, with scenes from the middle of the story, and this created a challenge for a slow starter like Jack: to shoot the first scene with a fully developed character that he had not had a chance to move around in and whose earlier relationship with other characters and circumstances hadn't yet been delineated. The director had held scene-by-scene rehearsals for a couple of weeks, but he stopped them because after a run-through or two, Jack would lose interest. This was largely owing to the fact that Jack's inclination is to refine a role rather than expand it. "Jack purifies his work shot after shot," Babenco says. "You never need to do more than four shots with him. After the third, he's brought his maximum. Even if you keep going, take eight is exactly like take three. Meryl is different. She can do eight takes of the same shot, and you get eight totally different performances."[25]

To launch the shoot, Babenco chose one of the scenes in which Jack and Streep work together. Their energy gave the initial push, "like putting a car in first gear" he said, because they "have a cult of admiration for each other." It was this cult of admiration that drew them to the work and that resulted in inspired performances. "Meryl and I have a very strong sense of acting collaboration and really enjoy working together," Jack said. "It has been true from the very first scene I ever did with her. She's very inspirational for me."[26] And Streep says of Jack, "He's a serious artist—I think he's a master. He's got a voracious appetite for work. He's never satisfied, but he's always churning. It's wild. There's nobody [else] out there that far in the movies. Nobody!"[27]

Both Jack and Meryl Streep were Oscar nominees for their roles in *Ironweed*, but neither won. The film played to critical acclaim, but perhaps owing to its subject matter, it didn't get the attention it deserved from moviegoers. Even so, it's one of those body-of-work films that will most certainly be taken into consideration whenever either of them is again nominated by the Academy.

The release of *Ironweed* was followed by *Broadcast News*, a hugely successful film about the television news business. In it, Jack did a cameo walk-on, portraying a superstar network anchorman whose bearing is reminiscent of television news star David Brinkley. Jack went unbilled in the film's promotion, and his brief but memorable appearance was both a surprise and a delight to most moviegoers. However, fans who were accustomed to his penchant for balancing his body of work—for his following a heavy, naturalistic portrayal like that of Francis Phelan in *Ironweed* with something as far removed from the portrayal as he could find—and who thought that *Broadcast News* was his change of pace were in for a surprise. He popped up next as a comic-book character, and the portrayal made him a very wealthy man.

As a child, Jack liked *Batman* because it was the only comic-book story that took place at night. Even so, he was not particularly taken with the idea of appearing in the Warner Brothers film. Coproducer Jon Peters, with whom Jack had worked in *Witches*, and whose idea it was to cast Michael Keaton in the role of Batman, approached Jack on the subject. Peters said that when he started telling Jack about the Joker, Jack almost threw him out of the room. Aside from the fact that it might be fun to play the Joker, there was little else about the role and the project that appealed to Jack, and much that gave him pause, not the least of which was the prospect of working with a thirty-year-old director, Tim Burton, who had done only two feature-length films, *Pee-wee's Big Adventure* and *Beetlejuice*. Both had made money and had shown Burton to be talented, but they weren't the kind of films Jack admired. He decided that he wanted to meet Burton first, "to see if we could get along," Jack said. Burton visited Jack's place in Aspen, Colorado, where they went horseback riding and got acquainted. Jack felt comfortable with him and said later that *Batman* was the most carefree production he had done. "I've even stopped watching dailies [the rough footage of the previous day's work]," he said during production. "At least half of what you see in dailies is junk, and you're always petrified that they're gonna pick the junk. But Tim and I like the same things, so I don't have to worry about it."[28] Jack's only advice to the young director before the shooting began was, "Just make sure you don't lose that old black-purple-night ominous feeling."[29] Burton didn't.

Batman was budgeted at about $30 million and was filmed in the winter of 1988 at Pinewood Studios outside London. The set was elaborate—a dark and foreboding Gothic "caricature" of New York City, called Gotham City—that was said to be the largest used since the filming of *Cleopatra*. The situation and characters were based on the adventures of comic-book hero Batman. Batman was created in 1939 by cartoonist Bob Kane, who served as a consultant on the film. The story concerns Bruce Wayne (Michael Keaton), who as a boy saw his parents mugged and murdered by thugs, and who as a decidedly neurotic man lives a double life. By day, he's a wealthy and prominent citizen; by night, he's a bat-costumed vigilante, waging battles against the forces of evil. His archnemesis in the film is Jack Napier (Jack), a petty gangster whom Batman throws into a vat of toxic waste and leaves for dead, but who emerges—after reconstructive surgery—as what writer Joe Morgenstern called a "deep-fried lunatic" known as the Joker. The Joker is a diabolical menace with a bone-white complexion, green hair, and a prosthetic, permanently etched fiendish smile. He refers to himself as "the world's first fully functioning homicidal artist." The plot concerns their battles and Batman's ultimate triumph.

It was Jack's show. Everyone liked him in the film, even though many critics and moviegoers, particularly the comic-book fans, were disappointed that the Joker played so large a part in it; they wanted to see more of Batman, more of his high-tech gadgets, Bat plane, and Batmobile. In effect, the Joker was the star, and only by making his part smaller could it have been otherwise. Like a circus clown drawing the crowd's attention from the staging area, Jack imbued the role with humor and shameless flamboyance, all teeth and white face and Day-Glo green hair and dazzling histrionics. Dressed in purple suits and orange shirts, he electrocuted people amid spectacular pyrotechnics and squirted acid in women's faces from his lapel flower, while Keaton, as the dark knight, was of necessity a hidden, shadowy figure. Keaton said later that to "out-outrageous" Jack in the film was simply impossible. He said that during the filming, Jack said to him, "Ya gotta let the wardrobe do the acting, kid."

It was this imbalance that the critics and many fans thought weakened the film. Still, it was judged by almost everyone as marvelously entertaining; this was evident when its theatrical rentals reached $250 million, one of the highest grossing films ever made.

It was also one of the most publicized and commercially exploited films ever made. The publicity campaign was launched early—even before the filming—exploiting what was alleged to be a Bat-fan outcry at the casting of Michael Keaton as their comic-book hero, and it ended long after the film had made its theatrical run, with stories that people feared the studio might not have enough video-cassettes of the film to meet the expected public demand (there were more than enough). In between was a deluge of material that told moviegoers more than they wanted to know not only about the film's stars, young director, budget, and sets but also about the history of Batman and other comic-book heroes and the optically illusive quality of the Batman logo. While all of this was being written and talked about, factories were gearing up for *Batman* products, including shoes, dolls, clothing, costumes, gadgets, toys, posters, jewelry, lunch boxes, and more—even a Batman breakfast cereal.

Meanwhile, Jack's accountants were also busy. His fee was now $6 million per picture and a percentage, off the top, of film-rental receipts. He had a similar arrangement for *Batman*, too, but it also included a percentage of *Batman*-product sales; thus his earnings from his participation in *Batman* have been estimated at between $30 and $60 million. As Jack said, seriously and in his singular manner, a year after the film's release, "I'm extremely financially viable."[30]

In 1989, without taking time off after *Batman*, Jack began his forty-fifth film, *The Two Jakes*—as its star, its coproducer, and its director. It was a project that haunted him almost as much as *Moontrap* obsesses him, one that caused a great deal of professional and personal anguish and a falling out among very close friends. *The Two Jakes* is a sequel to *Chinatown* and the second film of a proposed Los Angeles trilogy by Robert Towne, who won an Oscar for writing *Chinatown*. *The Two Jakes* takes place in 1948, a decade after the time of *Chinatown*, and is the continuing saga of Los Angeles private detective Jake Gittes (Jack) and his brushes with political power—the water industry in the first part, real estate and oil in this one.

The project began in late 1984 as a partnership to continue the trilogy, a partnership comprising only Jack, Towne, and their close mutual friend Robert Evans, the former Paramount production chief and actor who had produced *Chinatown*. Jack was to star in the film, Towne was to direct it from his own script, and Evans was to produce it and appear in it as Jake Berman, a real estate magnate (the other Jake in the story). They would own a large percentage of the picture, would not draw a fee or salary, and would split the profits. Paramount would handle the distribution. Then something happened; the exact nature of the problem is one of Hollywood's open but whispered secrets.

In April of 1985, three days before shooting was to begin and after the sets had been constructed and Paramount had spent about $3.5 million on the project, Robert Towne decided for reasons that have never been publicly disclosed that his friend Evans "wasn't up to the demands of the role" he had been set to play. Towne wanted him replaced.[31] Jack objected—particularly to the timing. He was sure Evans wouldn't willingly step out of the picture; they would look bad, and the studio would lose its millions if the project collapsed. Since Evans's scenes weren't scheduled until two weeks into the shooting, Jack said to Towne, "So let's ruthlessly shoot for two weeks and get Paramount on the hook for the picture, and we'll let Bobby [Evans] shoot a couple of days, and if he's no good, I'll support you in terms of replacing him, and then I think he will agree with it."[32] Jack figured that by following this course, Paramount would lose "maybe a hundred grand," representing the cost of recasting the part and reshooting the scenes, but they would save the millions it would otherwise cost them to close the picture down.

162 Even though Towne often publicly stated that he admired and respected Evans, he apparently felt that Evans was incapable of giving him the kind of performance he wanted, and he refused to go along with Jack's plan. The outcome was exactly as Jack had feared. Evans refused to relinquish the part, the partnership collapsed, and Paramount had to close the picture down. The sets, which had cost a million dollars, were struck and destroyed. Creditors filed suits against the three men, and their friendship was strained—perhaps irreparably.

One of the reasons Jack pushed "pigheadedly," he says, to revive *The Two Jakes* was to allay the rancor at its not having been made and to promote the possibility of a reconciliation among the friends. He speaks of people in the business who don't talk to one another owing to differences they've had over sometimes trivial moviemaking matters. "I didn't want big-time personal things in my life affected by making a movie," he said. "I had worked this long without that, and I wasn't about to let it happen now."[33] His relationship with Evans is good, but whether he and Towne have settled their differences is questionable. Jack admitted that the problems with the project had caused him personal discomfort and what he called "momentary cessations" in the friendships. As writer Joe Morgenstern observed, however, "It's hard to imagine that Towne was thrilled to see the direction of his script given over to Nicholson." This is particularly true when one considers that Towne originally had wanted to direct *Chinatown*, too, and since had directed other films. Morgenstern also noted that Towne, as the screenwriter, ordinarily would have been on the set with Jack at all times to do rewrites, which is customary. Instead, Towne left the country on vacation while Jack was shooting.

There was apparently no possibility of Robert Towne's directing *Jakes* after the project collapsed. Jack says that he approached three directors about replacing Towne: Roman Polanski, Bernardo Bertolucci, and John Huston. "But they couldn't do it," he said, "so there was no other director who could but me. The movie wouldn't have been made if I hadn't directed it. That's the main reason I did it, period."[34]

The Two Jakes was supposed to be released for the 1989 Christmas season, but was rescheduled for March 1990. Then a month before its rescheduled release date, Paramount announced that it would be released the following August. The reasons for the delay were never given, but insiders talked of problems with the editing and speculated that it might be Christmas 1990—a full year from its original release date—before the film would be ready. It was to be expected that Jack would take inordinate pains with the editing, as he had with *Drive, He Said,* for much was at stake beyond the $30 million production cost. As the sequel to a hugely popular and financially successful film, shot from the screenplay of an Oscar-winning writer, *The Two Jakes* was not only an intimidating challenge, but also Jack's greatest opportunity to gain recognition as a director. And this time the movie industry would be pulling for him. He knew that, and the pressure to succeed was intense.

The film was released in August 1990, and the reasons for its delay in release were evident in the viewing. Many reviewers said

163

that to appreciate *The Two Jakes* one had almost to see *Chinatown* again or first, despite the fact that Jack had added an opening narrative to give moviegoers a framework of reference—one that he wrote and delivered voiceover as Jake Gittes. But even when the film does manage to move away from the shadows of *Chinatown* into its own present tense, it does so listlessly and on a course that seems at times bewilderingly convoluted. It's an intelligent film with a fine cast and good moments, but critics considered it too dark and mannered and phlegmatic to attract a large audience. Their judgment proved accurate; *The Two Jakes* slipped through its play dates relatively unnoticed by most exhibitors and moviegoers.

It was characteristic of Jack to gamble with his reputation as a director on a vehicle that was heavy with excess baggage. And given the production's troubled, debilitating course, it's small wonder that reviewers found the battered director's effort confused and spiritless.

> "I hate feeling
> like I'm unac-
> ceptable be-
> cause of who I
> really am. I
> don't tell any-
> one the total
> truth."
>
> *Jack Nicholson*[1]

I n the first days of Jack Nicholson's life, he experienced the sort of impressions that must etch
indelibly in the psyche and exert a disturbing influence: feeling unwanted by his mother; feeling
an intruder in his own family. How could such an
irrational and absurd beginning not be a foun-
tainhead of fear, resentment, and rage? It's small
wonder that young Jack Nicholson shared Albert
Camus's views on the irrationality of life and the
absurdity of one's confronting it, or that he fer-
vently embraced that author's concept of the actor
as hero for living many lives through dramatic
portrayals. One would be hard pressed to imagine
philosophic tenets more compatible to a young
man born of Jack's circumstances and searching
for an identity and place. Small wonder, too, that
he found kindred spirits in bohemian Hollywood

18

DANCING ALONE

or that he clung to that lifestyle as though his identity and life depended upon it.

It's tempting to think of him as the personification of Camus's thesis: the "action writer," fashioning an acceptable persona in the likeness of Jack Nicholson and playing that role in a real-life script of his own devising, taking care to avoid scenes and relationships that might expose him as one whom even a mother wouldn't want. Jack loves to conjure small secrets and tuck them like hidden folds into the roles he plays on the screen. This would be his secret of secrets: that Jack Nicholson is merely a character that the real actor plays, the genie created by the boy.

So there he is, Jack Nicholson, an intellectual creation: the happy Irishman, keenly intelligent, generally kind, and fiercely loyal to his craft and to those he befriends. No one speaks unkindly of him, not even the women who loved him. He's artistic and fashion conscious—ablaze with color; he's sometimes a one-man Easter Parade. He's sentimental and generous, a lover of luxury and beauty, a collector of art and friends, wonderfully unpretentious. "His delight at being a famous movie star," says writer Leo Janos, "is so open, brassy, humor laden, and boldly outrageous as to make him one of the most genuinely loved characters in town."[2] Certainly, that's the way Jack wants to be and the way he is most of the time: appreciative of his good fortune and enjoying it, sharing it; burbling with blarney and charm; flashing that disarming smile. That smile, though, says writer Brad Darrach, is the kind that "gets one in the door but reveals nothing."[3]

If he could function always on that intellectual plane, all would be right with Jack's world. There are emotions to deal with, however, and emotions are not a function of the intellect; most of them are formed and still reside in that adolescent or childhood place.

So there he is, Jack the turbulent: guardedly watchful behind dark glasses, covering himself with fake behavior. Like his namesake, he's a gentle man who wards off the furies with chemicals. There are times, though, when the furies prevail. Then he's angry and seethingly vengeful, or remote and guarded. One can't get through to him; he will not be vulnerable. Writers who have occasion to interview him often reach for the "coiled-spring" metaphor to describe him, and sometimes note his extreme mood swings, his volatility—emotional highs and lows that are so intense as to make it impossible, Jack says, to keep up with him. He always gives the impression that he still regards himself an outsider. With Jack, it's me and them: longing to belong, while thumbing his nose and itching to get even with them for not belonging by birthright.

His anger rises—as do other unwanted emotions—from the well of his adolescence, and he sometimes indulges it adolescently: dropping his pants to moon a passing passenger train while on location for *The Last Detail*; dropping his pants to moon a crowd of tourists and locals who hounded him back aboard Sam Spiegel's yacht in France; railing still at the guys back in Neptune who lied to him decades ago about their sexual exploits. He is genuinely pleased when an interviewer suggests to him that today men assume he has more than his share of women, that he has many more affairs than he actually has, because he's a movie star. "That I like," Jack says, smiling broadly. "That part I don't mind. That's getting even."[4]

Some of his friends think that the turbulence, the dark moods, anger, vindictiveness, and what they call his "craziness" is due only to his Irish lineage. "He's Irish," writer Buck Henry has said. "He's got the demons."[5] Many see him as a "black-souled Irishman" who, when the klieg lights are off, thrashes about in the shadows of existential gloom. "When that Irish moodiness hit," Mimi Machu once said, "Jack would grab the back of his neck, throbbing with pain, and look as if he was boiling in oil."[6] Another of his friends was quoted as saying, "There's something Irish about his craziness. Jack's got a real hurt deep down inside, and there's no way of resolving it, ever."[7]

167

His approach to his work is not purely intellectual; the emotions poke through. He doesn't want them to because they're disruptive, but they do. One writer noted his "Contrariness, a sort of Peck's bad boyism, a certain brooding, stubborn determination to confound, not to be known, not to please, not to provide what is expected of him. The 'they' again: They think they know what they'll get from me; I'll show them."[8] The emotions show also in the work itself. More often than not, he chooses to play displaced persons. He feels compelled to choose these parts. As writer Kathleen Fury observed, his emotional attitudes are reflected also in the parts he chooses *not* to play. Since *Easy Rider*, he has had the luxury of choosing his own roles, his own scripts, and, as Fury notes, "he has never chosen an uncomplicated romantic situation between a man and a woman, a story of passionate love or enduring companionship."[9] He has never chosen such a role in his personal life, either.

By mid-1987, Jack's fifteen-year romance with Anjelica had ended. The dissolution wasn't sudden; it probably began unintentionally with Anjelica's decision in 1981 to make a career of acting and with her move from the Mulholland Drive house. Jack could not have been more supportive of her career decision, but it must have troubled him. He has had brief affairs with actresses, but he has made a conscious effort to avoid serious involvements with them because show-business marriages are difficult to maintain. The fact that Anjelica got involved in her own career and was no longer always available for him undoubtedly became a matter of contention and probably contributed to their breakup, but it was by no means the cause of it.

Anjelica had moved from Jack's house and had begun her career out of a need to get on with a life of her own. This need must have risen from the sad realization that her relationship with Jack had reached a dead end long before. They had separated many times previously, but friends had noted signs of finality in this one: Anjelica bought a house of her own; Jack didn't accompany her to the Emmy Awards when she was nominated for her role in the Western film *Lonesome Dove*, which was released as a television miniseries; then John Huston died. Huston was the last of Jack's elder mentors. Shorty, Orson Welles, and Sam Spiegel were gone, too. Jack had said that when Huston died he'd "cry forever." But the night before Huston's funeral, Jack wasn't there for Anjelica—perhaps because she no longer wanted him there. These were the kind of events that in the past surely would have brought them back together.

Like Mimi Machu and Michelle Phillips, Anjelica had come to realize that while Jack can be an exciting—if exasperating—man and a loyal and charming friend, what you see is what you get—on his terms. He is difficult to live with, and quite incapable of opening up, of giving himself completely. He will share parts of his life and himself; he will even marry if that's what it takes to maintain possession of the woman in his life, but that really will not change anything; a wife will still have to take a number and wait in line. She may be number one, but there will still be a line and other numbers. All the women in Jack's life must have assumed that he would change, must have thought him a late bloomer who would eventually blossom, mature. And all of them were worn down emotionally from trying to deal with him. Anjelica had been the most patient of them, the most malleable. She had found it exciting to leave the rigors of modeling and to live Jack's life with him. Had his frequent marriage proposals represented an emotional commitment to her—rather than a need to hold her in place—she would surely have married him. However, marriage was something Jack would give, not share; he would even sacrifice himself on the altar of matrimony to keep from being left again.

This is not to say that Jack didn't love Anjelica—or Mimi or Michelle. He did. One is reminded, however, of his role as Garrett Breedlove in *Terms of Endearment,* a characterization that may be as close to the real Jack Nicholson as any he has played. When Aurora asks in the film how he would respond if she declared her love for him, Breedlove says he'd have to give his stock reply: "I love you, too, kid!" He says this without a trace of sincerity, then, flashing a smile that reveals nothing, he turns and walks out of her life.

The role of mate in Jack's scenario is not a costarring one, but a supporting one, with alluring understudies in the wings; yet the kind of woman to whom he is most attracted—the fiery, independent type who keep his socks in the sink—is the least likely to tolerate his adolescent behavior or the subordinate role he casts her in. He identified with playwright Eugene O'Neill in this respect, and apparently envied O'Neill's finding a woman who "more or less just eliminated the romance and just sort of managed him."

Nothing less than a total, irreparable, and perhaps rancorous rupture in his relationship with Anjelica would have launched Jack into the kind of eccentric orbit he then followed, one reminiscent of that after his breakup with Sandra. He had, of course, chased after women all the while he was living with Anjelica. Out of deference to her, he had tried—in his fashion—to be discreet and to keep his flings brief and casual, however. That pattern changed drastically in the late 1980s.

"After three decades and 40-plus pictures," a magazine reported in December 1989, "Nicholson has become that rare public figure whose art permits him to float, beloved and bankable, almost beyond criticism or scandal."[10] The reference was to Jack's publicized involvement with two actresses, Rebecca Broussard and Karen Mayo-Chandler. The nature of the involvements signaled that he was on the loose again, making up for lost time, and that he was renewing his efforts to achieve a goal he had presumably abandoned during his years with Anjelica.

On Monday, April 16, 1990, Rebecca Broussard gave birth to a daughter by Jack at Cedars-Sinai Medical Center in Los Angeles; she was named Lorraine Broussard Nicholson, presumably after Jack's aunt Lorraine, and her birth was announced by Jack and Rebecca through Jack's publicist, Paul Wasserman. Broussard is a twenty-six-year-old actress who played the part of Jack's secretary in *The Two Jakes* and who is said to have met him while working as a waitress at Helena's, a Los Angeles night spot in which Jack has a financial interest. It was reported that Jack had settled Broussard in a $3 million home in Beverly Hills a few months before the baby was born and that he opened a $200,000 bank account for her and the child. There were apparently no marriage plans.

Jack's arrangement with Broussard was the kind he had tried to establish with other women prior to his relationship with Anjelica. He had often said in interviews that the idea of having more children appealed to him and that it was one of the goals he regretted not pursuing more diligently. He has his daughter, Jennifer, of course, and there was a son, Caleb, born to actress Susan Anspach. He wanted more children, though. He said years earlier that he'd like to have six more children by other women and that if he could "redesign the universe," he would "make it possible for people to live out that fantasy."[11] He told writer Kathleen Fury fifteen years earlier of his efforts to bring more offspring into the world. "I've actually proposed it on occasion to women I've known," he said. "You know, however they'd want to do it—either I'd take the child or they would." Thinking of an offspring's emotional welfare in such circumstances, Fury told Jack that she thought he was crazy. However, the basis of her concern was not apparent to him. "No, I'm not," he said. "I can afford it, darling. Don't you understand? I'm actually in a position to carry it off."[12]

What is most curious about his proposal and subsequent action is that he is carrying it off despite the fact that he apparently considers it a terrible handicap that he was, himself, illegitimately born. He tried for years to keep the fact from the public, and he has publicly decried the stigma that attaches to illegitimacy, calling it "still the heaviest prejudice in the world" and saying that there are no "Jackie Robinsons" to break the illegitimacy barrier as Robinson had broken the color barrier in baseball. Once, when accused of being a male chauvinist for undermining the women's movement with the movie roles he chooses to play, he replied, "I have my own favorite downtrodden minority, and it's not women. It's the bastard, the illegitimately born."[13] He made the statement a year after he revealed his desire to bring more illegitimate children into the world.

Shortly after the fact of Rebecca Broussard's pregnancy was made public, another woman, whom Jack apparently had approached unsuccessfully earlier with the idea of bearing his child, made her affair with him known. She was former British model and actress Karen Mayo-Chandler, who posed for the December 1989 issue of *Playboy* magazine and told of a "year-long" affair with Jack in 1987, prior to the filming of *Batman.* Mayo-Chandler also had met Rebecca Broussard, but she made it clear that she was unwilling to join her on maternity row. Besides detailing her bedroom antics with Jack, Mayo-Chandler commented on the idea of bearing Jack's children. "For me," she said, "Jack was not a suitable candidate because of the major age difference. I want it to be somebody to grow old with me and still be young when the child is an adult."[14] She also revealed that on the night before John Huston's funeral, Jack invited her up to his place on Mulholland Drive. "I had to wonder," she said, "why he wasn't consoling Anjelica instead of making love to me. My God, he was passionate that night."[15]

While preparing to write an article about Jack in the mid-1970s, writer Kathleen Fury asked two unidentified female friends their impressions of him. "A very sexy man," one said, "but I wouldn't want to get too involved with him; there's a little boy sensitivity about him that I suspect might be very destructive to women." The other said: "When Nicholson's on the screen, I usually don't watch anyone else. Such *intensity.* But there's also something, I don't know . . . adolescent."[16]

Author Jeremy Larner, who cowrote the screen adaptation of his novel *Drive, He Said* with Jack and who worked with him on location, once was asked to briefly characterize Nicholson. Larner likened Jack to Jay Gatsby, the protagonist of F. Scott Fitzgerald's novel.[17] He used a quote from the book that is remarkably poignant even in its details if one bears in mind that Jack spent the summers of his youth in Stony Brook, Long Island, in what he called a "very nice upper-class atmosphere" and that he escaped being known "only as Jackie Nicholson" by leaving home at age seventeen on Lorraine's advice:

> The truth was that Jay Gatsby of West Egg, Long Island, sprang from his Platonic conception of himself. He was the son of God—a phrase which, if it means anything, means just that —and he must be about His Father's business, the service of a vast, vulgar, and meretricious beauty. So he invented just the sort of Jay Gatsby that a seventeen-year-old boy would be likely to invent, and to this conception he was faithful to the end.[18]

Jack has found his place on Mulholland Drive—a place high above Hollywood and above everyone in Hollywood except Marlon Brando. A safe place. "You could come through this house and not find out a thing about me," he told an interviewer.[19] He has since made it a safer place. "I stopped by Jack's house not long ago," actor Nick Nolte said, "just goofing around. The whole street's locked up. I punched the button on the big iron gate. Lights came on; cameras started to roll; a voice came out: 'Who are you? What do you want?' I said, 'Is Jack there?' The voice said, 'It's four in the morning, pal.' I said, 'Oh, oh, okay.' The cameras were still going when I left."[20]

Inside, when there is no company at night, Jack has a habit of putting on rock music so loudly that it rips from the speakers. Then he sometimes lights a joint and in the reflection of the wide glass doors that overlook the dark canyon below, he dances, alone.

Chapter 1: Family Secret—1974

1. Richard Warren Lewis, *Playboy*, April 1972, p. 78 (interview).
2. Nancy Collins, "The Great Seducer, Jack Nicholson," *Rolling Stone*, March 29, 1984, p. 17.
3. Ovid Demaris, "Is Jack Nicholson Hiding Something?" *Parade*, January 1, 1984, p. 17. The facts of Nicholson's birth were first published in this article. Demaris quotes Nicholson as saying, "Actually, I'm surprised that you've heard about it [the family secret] because I made a personal decision when I got this information some 10 years ago: since I can't figure out how many of my friends know about it, I decided not to talk about it."
4. Nicholson has told several interviewers, in-

cluding Leo Janis (*Cosmopolitan,* December 1976) and Jack Cocks (*Time,* August 12, 1974), that June had left home when he was four; he told several others, including Chris Chase (*Cosmopolitan,* February 1983) and Nancy Collins (*Rolling Stone,* March 28, 1984), that she was sixteen or seventeen when she left.

5. Richard Warren Lewis, op. cit., p. 78.
6. Brad Darrach, "Jack Is Nimble, Jack Is Best . . .," *People,* December 8, 1975, p. 54.

Chapter 2: Neptune City and Spring Lake

1. Ovid Demaris, "Is Jack Nicholson Hiding Something?" *Parade,* January 1, 1984, p. 16.
2. *Ritz* (British magazine), number 88, June 1984, p. 19. In this uncredited London interview, Nicholson said, "I was born in Manhattan and grew up in New Jersey." Also, Chris Chase of *The New York Times* quotes him on February 5, 1982, as saying, "Now I've returned here [New York City] to the city of my birth."
3. Richard Warren Lewis, *Playboy,* April 1972, p. 89 (interview).
4. Jay Cocks, "The Star with the Killer Smile," *Time,* August 12, 1974, p. 48.
5. Martin Torgoff, "Making Out on Mulholland Drive," *Interview,* August 1984, p. 48.
6. Fred Schruers, *Rolling Stone,* August 14, 1986, p. 48 (interview).
7. Ovid Demaris, op. cit., p. 16.
8. Kathlene D. Fury, "Jack Nicholson," *Ladies' Home Journal,* April 1976, p. 185.
9. Jack has revealed only that June had two children; their sex is unknown.
10. Fred Schruers, op. cit., p. 49.
11. Ron Rosenbaum, "The Method and Mystique of Jack Nicholson," *The New York Times Magazine,* July 13, 1986, p. 20.
12. Leo Janos, "Jack Nicholson: Bankable and Brilliant," *Cosmopolitan,* December 1976, p. 181.

Chapter 3: Subterranean Hollywood

1. John Gilmore, from a personal interview.
2. Martin Torgoff, "Making Out on Mulholland Drive," *Interview*, August 1984, p. 48.
3. According to his certificate of death, John Joseph Nicholson died on July 24, 1955, at age fifty-seven of acute cardiovascular disease and cancer of the sigmoid colon.
4. Richard Warren Lewis, *Playboy*, April 1972, p. 82 (interview).
5. Ibid. Jack included actor Dennis Hopper in his remarks, saying, "Actually, Dennis and I originally became actors because we like parties." Jack was presumptuous in speaking for Hopper, who had been under contract to Warner Brothers and who was intensely serious about the art of acting—even obsessed with it. Hopper strove to be an actor, not merely a performer. He was unrestrained in his approach to the art and worked as close to the precarious edge as his talent would take him.
6. John Gilmore, op. cit.
7. Richard Warren Lewis, op. cit., p. 86.
8. Richard Warren Lewis, op. cit., p. 82.
9. Jamie Wolf, "It's All Right, Jack," *American Film*, January–February 1984, p. 37.

Chapter 4: The Professional

1. Rex Reed, "The Man Who Walked Off with *Easy Rider*," *The New York Times*, March 1, 1970, p. 13.
2. Tom Shales, "Shore Patrol for Jack Nicholson," *The Los Angeles Times*, March 1, 1973, p. 22.
3. Sandra Knight was born September 2, 1939, in Pennsylvania, the daughter of Herbert and Brida Knight (née Harvey).
4. An interview with Roger Corman in Robert David Crane and Christopher Fryer, *Jack Nicholson Face to Face* (New York: M. Evans and Company, 1975), p. 25.

Chapter 5: Troubled Years

1. Jay Cocks, "The Star with the Killer Smile," *Time*, August 12, 1974, p. 49.

2. The exact date of June's death is unknown, but she died in late 1963. Jack will discuss her only in a general way and has not revealed her married name, so her public records are not readily available.
3. Nancy Collins, "The Great Seducer, Jack Nicholson," *Rolling Stone*, March 29, 1984, p. 17.
4. Ibid.
5. David Downing, *Jack Nicholson* (New York: Stein and Day, 1984), p. 34.
6. Ibid.

Chapter 6: On the Rocks

1. John Gilmore, from a personal interview.
2. Kathleen D. Fury, "Jack Nicholson," *Ladies' Home Journal*, April 1976, p. 186.
3. Ibid.
4. Robert David Crane and Christopher Fryer, *Jack Nicholson Face to Face* (New York: M. Evans and Company, 1975), p. 126.
5. Ibid., p. 46.
6. Ibid., p. 17
7. Ibid., p. 26
8. Ibid., p. 37
9. John Gilmore, op. cit.
10. David Downing, *Jack Nicholson* (New York: Stein and Day, 1984), p. 53.
11. Ibid.

Chapter 7: Through the Looking Glass

1. Richard Warren Lewis, *Playboy*, April 1972, p. 80, (interview).
2. John Gilmore, from a personal interview.
3. An interview with Richard Rush in Robert D. Crane and Christopher Fryer, *Jack Nicholson Face to Face*, (New York: M. Evans and Company, 1975), p. 38.
4. John Gilmore, op. cit.
5. An interview with Dennis Hopper in Crane and Fryer, op. cit., p. 73.

6. Ibid., p. 79.
7. Ibid., p. 100.
8. Richard Warren Lewis, op. cit., p. 80.
9. Ibid.
10. Crane and Fryer, op. cit., p. 47.
11. Chris Chase, "Nicholson: The Legend That Jack Built," *Cosmopolitan*, February 1983, p. 171.
12. Stephen Schiff, "Jumping Jack," *Vanity Fair*, August 1986, p. 65.

Chapter 8: Changes

1. Kathleen D. Fury, "Jack Nicholson," *Ladies' Home Journal*, April 1976, p. 188.
2. Leo Janos "Jack Nicholson: Bankable and Brilliant," *Cosmopolitan*, December 1976, p. 180.
3. According to her death certificate, Ethel May Nicholson died at 6:45 P.M. on January 6, 1970, at the Geraldine L. Thompson Medical Home at Allenwood, New Jersey, of Deamato myositis and chronic myocarditis, complicated by diabetes and osteoporosis. She was buried January 10, 1970, at Monmoth Park in New Shrewsbury, New Jersey.
4. Richard Warren Lewis, *Playboy*, April 1972, p. 89 (interview).
5. Tag Gallagher, "Jack Nicholson, Easy Actor," *The Village Voice*, June 9, 1975, p. 79.
6. Rex Reed, "The Man Who Walked Off with *Easy Rider,"The New York Times*, March 1, 1970, p. 22.
7. Ibid.
8. Ibid.
9. Ron Rosenbaum, "The Method and Mystique of Jack Nicholson," *The New York Times Magazine*, July 13, 1986, p. 19.
10. Jay Cocks "The Star with the Killer Smile," *Time*, August 12, 1974, p. 47.
11. Ron Rosenbaum, op. cit., p. 19
12. An item unsigned in the March 1980 issue of *Playgirl* said, in part: "Speaking of Jack Nicholson, he and actress Susan Anspach have finally admitted in public what their friends have known for years—that Susan's son is Jack's child, conceived

while they were filming *Five Easy Pieces* several years ago. Neither wanted to marry at the time, although Jack always privately acknowledged that the child was his."

13. Nancy Collins, "The Great Seducer, Jack Nicholson," *Rolling Stone*, March 29, 1984, p. 18.
14. Ibid., p. 119.

Chapter 9: New Directions

1. Douglas Brode, *The Films of Jack Nicholson* (Secaucus, New Jersey: Citadel Press, 1987), p. 124.
2. Robert David Crane and Christopher Fryer, *Jack Nicholson Face to Face* (New York: M. Evans and Company, 1975), p. 48.
3. Ibid., p. 31.
4. Guy Flatley, "Jack Nicholson—Down to the Very *Last Detail*," *The New York Times*, February 10, 1974, p. D11.
5. Jamie Wolf, "It's All Right, Jack," *American Film*, January–February 1984, p. 32.
6. Crane and Fryer, op. cit., p. 53.
7. Leo Janos, "Jack Nicholson: Bankable and Brilliant," *Cosmopolitan*, December 1976, p. 180.
8. Richard Warren Lewis, *Playboy*, April 1972, p. 86 (interview).
9. Ibid., p. 88.
10. Crane and Fryer, op. cit., p. 54.
11. Tom Shales, "Shore Patrol Duty for Jack Nicholson," *Los Angeles Times*, March 1, 1973, p. 22.

Chapter 10: Anjelica

1. Brad Darrach, "Jack Finds His Queen of Hearts," *People*, July 8, 1985, p. 56.
2. Joan Juliet Buck, "Anjelica Huston: A Born Knock-Out," *Vogue*, September 1985, p. 676.
3. Brad Darrach, op. cit., p. 56.
4. Ibid.

Chapter 11: Beyond Stardom

1. Douglas Brode, *The Films of Jack Nicholson* (Secaucus, New Jersey: Citadel Press, 1987).
2. Ibid.
3. Tag Gallagher, "Jack Nicholson, Easy Actor" *The Village Voice*, June 9, 1975, p. 80.
4. Ibid, p. 80.
5. Ron Rosenbaum, "The Method and Mystique of Jack Nicholson," *The New York Times Magazine*, July 13, 1986, p. 17.
6. Crane and Fryer, op. cit., p. 122

Chapter 12: Mr. Brando and Other Problems

1. Leo Janos, "Jack Nicholson: Bankable and Brilliant," *Cosmopolitan*, December 1976, p. 180.
2. Tag Gallagher, "Jack Nicholson, Easy Actor," *The Village Voice*, June 9, 1975, p. 80.
3. Leo Janos, op. cit., p. 78.
4. Bill Davidson, "The Conquering Antihero," *The New York Times Magazine*, October 12, 1975.
5. One example of Brando's misinterpreted reference appeared in David Thompson's article (*Playgirl*, April 1981), in which Thompson said, "Moreover, in an Italian interview Brando made teasing allusions to the possibility of a gay affair between himself and Nicholson—something Nicholson stolidly ignored or denied, thereby picking up the pattern of innocent cowboy and demonic charlatan established in the film."
6. Leo Janos, op. cit., p. 180.
7. Nancy Collins, "The Great Seducer, Jack Nicholson" *Rolling Stone*, March 29, 1984, p. 20.
8. Unsigned item, *People*, August 16, 1976.
9. Bill Davidson, op. cit.
10. Leo Janos, op. cit., p. 178.

Chapter 13: The Curse of Answered Prayers

1. Martin Torgoff, "Making Out on Mulholland Drive," *Interview*, August 1984, p. 48.

2. Fred Schruers, An Interview, *Rolling Stone,* August 14, 1986, p. 50.
3. Stephen Schiff, "Jumping Jack," *Vanity Fair,* August 1986, p. 65.
4. Robert David Crane and Christopher Fryer, "Jack Nicholson," *Genesis,* February 1975, p. 43.
5. Tag Gallagher, "Jack Nicholson, Easy Actor," *The Village Voice,* June 9, 1975, p. 80.
6. Stephen Schiff, op. cit., p. 62.
7. David Downing, *Jack Nicholson* (New York: Stein and Day, 1984), p. 107.
8. Brad Darrach, "Jack Is Nimble, Jack Is Best . . . ," *People,* December 8, 1975, p. 52.
9. Tag Gallagher, op. cit., p. 79.
10. Jamie Wolf, "It's All Right, Jack," *American Film,* January– February 1984, p. 36.

Chapter 14: Over the Top

1. Jamie Wolf, "It's All Right Jack," *American Film,* January– February 1984, p. 32:
2. Chris Chase, "Nicholson: The Legend That Jack Built," *Cosmopolitan,* February 1983, p. 254.
3. Ibid.
4. Bob Woodward, *Wired: The Short Life and Fast Times of John Belushi* (New York: Simon and Schuster, 1984), p. 136.
5. Jamie Wolf, op. cit., p. 32.
6. Douglas Brode, *The Films of Jack Nicholson* (Secaucus, New Jersey: Citadel Press, 1987), p. 201.
7. Bob Woodward, op. cit., p. 151.
8. Ibid.
9. Jamie Wolf, "It's All Right, Jack." *American Film,* January– February 1984, p. 37.

Chapter 15: Mulholland Man

1. Martin Torgoff, "Making Out on Mulholland Drive," *Interview,* August 1984, p. 46.

2. David Thomson, "Jack Nicholson, King of Mulholland," *Playgirl*, April 1981, p. 38.
3. Richard Warren Lewis, *Playboy*, April 1972, p. 76 (interview).
4. Martin Torgoff, op. cit., p. 46.
5. Richard Warren Lewis, op. cit., p. 78.
6. Brad Darrach,"Jack Is Nimble, Jack Is Best . . . ," *People*, December 8, 1975, p. 54.
7. Bob Woodward, *Wired, the Short Life and Fast Times of John Belushi* (New York: Simon and Schuster, 1984), p. 122.
8. Ibid., p. 315.
9. Ibid., p. 356.
10. Peter Lester, *People*, July 28, 1980, p. 74.
11. Gregg Kilday, "Jack Nicholson's Face Odysseys," *Gentleman's Quarterly*, March 1981, p. 180.
12. Chris Chase, "Nicholson: The Legend That Jack Built," *Cosmopolitan*, February 1983, p. 253.
13. Martin Torgoff, op. cit., p. 46.
14. Ibid.
15. *Ritz* (British magazine), number 88, June 1984, p. 19. The interviewer is identified only as David.
16. Nancy Collins, "The Great Seducer, Jack Nicholson," *Rolling Stone*, March 29, 1984, p. 18.

Chapter 16: On the Edge

181

1. Nancy Collins, "The Great Seducer, Jack Nicholson," *Rolling Stone*, March 29, 1984, p. 18.
2. Gregg Kilday,"Jack Nicholson's Face Odysseys," *Gentleman's Quarterly*, March 1981, p. 179.
3. Roderick Mann, *The Los Angeles Times*, October 3, 1978.
4. Ibid.
5. Douglas Brode, *The Films of Jack Nicholson* (Secaucus, New Jersey: Citadel Press, 1987), p. 208.
6. David Downing, *Jack Nicholson* (New York: Stein and Day, 1984), p. 154.
7. Ibid.
8. Douglas Brode, op. cit., p. 208.

9. Roderick Mann, *The Los Angeles Times Calendar*, February 21, 1982, p. 34.
10. Chris Chase, "Nicholson: The Legend That Jack Built" *Cosmopolitan*, February 1983, p. 170.
11. Roderick Mann, op. cit., p. 34.
12. Nancy Collins, op. cit., p. 20.
13. Douglas Brode, op. cit., p. 224.
14. Roderick Mann, op. cit., p. 34.
15. Ibid.
16. Fred Schruers, "An Interview," *Rolling Stone*, August 14, 1986, p. 48.

Chapter 17: Breaking Hard

1. Jamie Wolf,"It's All Right, Jack," *American Film*, January–February 1984, p. 37.
2. Chris Chase, *The New York Times*, February 5, 1982, p. C8.
3. Jamie Wolf, op. cit., p. 36.
4. Roderick Mann, *The Los Angeles Times Calendar*, February 21, 1982, p. 34.
5. Nancy Collins,"The Great Seducer, Jack Nicholson," *Rolling Stone*, March 29, 1984, p. 20.
6. Among Brooks's successful television series of the day were "The Mary Tyler Moore Show," "Rhoda," and "Taxi."
7. Stephen Farber, *The Los Angeles Herald Examiner*, November 27, 1983, p. E1.
8. Ovid Demaris,"Is Jack Nicholson Hiding Something?" *Parade*, January 1, 1984, p. 17.
9. Joan Juliet Buck, "Anjelica Huston: A Born Knock-Out," *Vogue*, September 1985, p. 749.
10. Douglas Brode, *The Films of Jack Nicholson* (Secaucus, New Jersey: Citadel Press, 1987), p. 242.
11. Brad Darrach, "Jack Finds His Queen of Hearts," *People*, July 8, 1985, p. 56.
12. Brad Darrach, op. cit., p. 57.
13. Douglas Brode, op. cit., p. 244.
14. Stephen Schiff,"Jumping Jack," *Vanity Fair*, August 1986, p. 62.
15. Ibid. p. 64.
16. Ibid.

17. Ron Rosenbaum, "The Method and Mystique of Jack Nicholson," *The New York Times Magazine*, July 13, 1986, p. 49.
18. Ibid. p. 15.
19. Ibid. p. 16.
20. Douglas Brode, op. cit., p. 253.
21. Ibid.
22. Ibid, p. 254.
23. Ibid.
24. David Rensin, "Shot by Shot," *Premiere*, January 1988, p. 56.
25. Ibid.
26. Ibid.
27. Uncredited, *People*, December 25–January 1, 1990, p. 48.
28. Jack Kroll, "Return to Gotham City," *Newsweek*, January 23, 1988, p. 68.
29. Ibid.
30. Joe Morgenstern, "Remember It, Jack, It's Chinatown," *Gentleman's Quarterly*, January 1990, p. 131.
31. Ibid, p. 175.
32. Ibid.
33. Ibid, p. 133
34. Joe Morgenstern, op. cit., p. 175.

Chapter 18: Dancing Alone

1. Kathleen D. Fury, "Jack Nicholson," *Ladies' Home Journal*, April 1976, p. 189.
2. Leo Janos, "Jack Nicholson: Bankable and Brilliant," *Cosmopolitan*, December 1976, p. 178.
3. Brad Darrach, "Jack Is Nimble, Jack Is Best . . . ," *People*, December 8, 1975, p. 52.
4. Nancy Collins, "The Great Seducer, Jack Nicholson," *Rolling Stone*, March 29, 1984, p. 17.
5. Jamie Wolf, "It's All Right, Jack," *American Film*, January–February 1984, p. 37.
6. Leo Janos, op. cit., p. 180.
7. Nancy Collins, op. cit., p. 17.
8. Jamie Wolf, op. cit., p. 37.
9. Kathleen D. Fury, op. cit., p. 186.
10. Uncredited, *People*, December 25–January 1, 1990, p. 48.

11. Kathleen D. Fury, op cit., p. 189.
12. Ibid.
13. Bill Davidson, "The Conquering Antihero," *The New York Times Magazine*, October 12, 1975.
14. Jeannie Williams, "Jack as a Fling, But Not a Father," *USA Today*, October 30, 1989, p. D-2.
15. Ibid.
16. Kathleen D. Fury, op. cit., p. 94.
17. An interview with Jeremy Larner in Robert David Crane and Christopher Fryer, *Jack Nicholson Face to Face* (New York: M. Evans and Company, 1975), p. 44.
18. F. Scott Fitzgerald, *The Great Gatsby* (New York: Charles Scribner's Sons, 1925).
19. Martin Torgoff, "Making Out on Mulholland Drive," *Interview*, August 1984, p. 46.
20. Chris Chase, "Nicholson: The Legend That Jack Built," *Cosmopolitan*, February 1983, p. 169.

184

The following is a chronological listing of films in which Jack Nicholson has appeared, together with release companies and dates, selected credits, and relevant biographical matter. These are followed by lists of films that he wrote, directed, and coproduced.

1. *The Cry Baby Killer* (Allied Artists release, 1958). Director, Jus Addis; Screenplay, Leo Gordon and Melvin Levy; Cinematographer, Floyd Crosby; *Cast includes*: Harry Lauter, Jack Nicholson, Brett Halsey, Carolyn Mitchell, Lynn Cartwright, John Shay, Jordan Whitfield, Roger Corman, Leo Gordon. Shot in ten days for seven thousand dollars, this was Jack's first film and a starring role, made three years after he moved to California. Though it seemed a promising start, he didn't

FILMOGRAPHY

find work in films again for almost two years. He plays seventeen-year-old Jimmy Walker, who is attacked by three teenage toughs at a drive-in restaurant. Thinking he has killed two of them in self-defense with their own gun (they're only wounded), he takes hostages. All ends well.

2. *The Little Shop of Horrors* (The Filmgroup release, 1960). Director, Roger Corman; Screenplay, Charles B. Griffith; Cinematographer, Archie Dalzell; *Cast includes*: Jonathan Haze, Jackie Joseph, Mel Welles, Myrtle Vail, Jack Nicholson. This send-up of horror films is available on videocassette and is cherished by film buffs. It was produced by Roger Corman for $22,500; Warner Brothers bought the remake rights in 1984 for a reported half a million dollars and made it into a musical. Jack does a very funny bit part as a masochistic dental patient.

3. *Too Soon to Love* (Universal-International release, 1960). Director, Richard Rush; Screenplay, Lazlo Gorog and Richard Rush; Cinematographer, William Thompson; *Cast includes*: Jennifer West, Richard Evans, Warren Parker, Ralph Manza, Jack Nicholson. The story of an unwed teenage couple's unwanted pregnancy and its social complications. Jack plays the young man's friend.

4. *Studs Lonigan* (United Artists release, 1960). Director, Irving Lerner; Screenplay, Philip Yordan, from novelist James T. Farrell's trilogy; Cinematographer, Arthur Feindel; *Cast includes*: Christopher Knight, Frank Gorshin, Venetia Stevenson, Carolyn Craig, Jack Nicholson. The story of a youth's disillusionment in 1920s Chicago. Jack plays weary Reilly, a member of Stud's youth gang.

5. *The Wild Ride* (The Filmgroup release, 1960). Director, Harvey Berman; Screenplay, Ann Porter and Marion Rothman; Cinematographer, Taylor Sloan; *Cast includes*: Jack Nicholson, Georgianna Carter, Robert Bean. The story of Johnny Varron (Jack), a ruthless hot rod–gang leader whose recklessness causes numerous automobile fatalities.

6. *The Broken Land* (Twentieth Century-Fox release, 1962). Director, John Bushelman; Screenplay, Edward Lakso; Cinematographer, Floyd Crosby; *Cast includes*: Kent Taylor, Dianna Darrin, Jody McCrea, Robert Sampson, Jack Nicholson, Gary

Snead. Jack plays the son of a famous gunfighter in a town dominated by a sadistic marshal.

7. *The Raven* (American International Pictures release, 1963). Director, Roger Corman; Screenplay, Richard Matheson; Cinematographer, Floyd Crosby; *Cast includes*: Vincent Price, Peter Lorre, Boris Karloff, Hazel Court, Olive Sturgess, Jack Nicholson, Connie Wallace, William Baskin, Aaron Saxon. Jack plays Peter Lorre's son in this comedy thriller that many critics found amusing.

8. *The Terror* (American International Pictures release, 1963). Director, Roger Corman; Screenplay, Leo Gordon and Jack Hill; Cinematographer, John Nickolaus, Jr.; *Cast includes*: Boris Karloff, Jack Nicholson, Sandra Knight, Richard Miller, Dorothy Neumann, Jonathan Haze. Jack plays an officer of Napoleon's army who is stranded on a Baltic shore and wanders into a castle in search of a girl who helped him. The girl is Jack's then wife, Sandra Knight; this is the only film they appeared in together. She retired from acting.

9. *Ensign Pulver* (Warner Brothers release, 1964). Director, Joshua Logan; Screenplay, Joshua Logan and Peter S. Feibleman; Cinematographer, Charles Lawton; *Cast includes*: Robert Walker, Jr., Burl Ives, Walter Matthau, Millie Perkins, Tommy Sands, Larry Hagman, Jack Nicholson. Jack plays a bit part as a seaman. His mother, June, died while he was en route to Mexico to do this film; his daughter was born the day he returned.

10. *Back Door to Hell* (Twentieth Century-Fox release, 1964). Director, Monte Hellman; Screenplay, Richard Guttman and John Hackett; Cinematographer, Mars Rasca; *Cast includes*: Jimmie Rodgers, Jack Nicholson, Annabelle Huggins, Conrad Maga, Johnny Monteiro, Joe Sison. Jack plays a soldier named Burnett, a member of a three-man reconnaissance team that lands in the Philippine Islands prior to the U.S. invasion during World War Two. Filmed in the Philippines.

11. *Flight to Fury* (Twentieth Century-Fox release, 1966). Director, Monte Hellman; Screenplay, Jack Nicholson; Cinematographer, Mike Accion; *Cast includes*: Dewey Martin, Fay Spain, Jack Nicholson, Jacqueline Hellman, Vic Diaz, Joseph Estrada, John Hackett, Juliet Prado. Jack plays a psychopathic killer on

a murderous quest for a pouch of smuggled diamonds. This is the second of his six credits as a screenwriter—*Thunder Island*, in which he did not appear, was his first.

12. *The Shooting* (Jack H. Harris release, 1966). Director, Monte Hellman; Screenplay, Adrien Joyce (Carol Eastman); Cinematographer, Gregory Sandor; *Cast includes:* Warren Oates, Will Hutchins, Millie Perkins, Jack Nicholson, B. J. Merholz, Cuy El Tsosie, Charles Eastman. Jack plays a gunfighter in this existential Western, which he coproduced with Monte Hellman.

13. *Ride in the Whirlwind* (Jack H. Harris release, 1966). Director, Monte Hellman; Screenplay, Jack Nicholson; Cinematographer, Gregory Sandor; *Cast includes:* Cameron Mitchell, Jack Nicholson, Millie Perkins, Tom Filer, Katherine Squire, George Mitchell, Brandon Carroll. Jack's third screenwriting credit. He plays one of three cowboys who are mistaken for outlaws and hunted. The second of the two interesting existential Westerns he coproduced with Monte Hellman.

14. *Hell's Angels on Wheels* (U.S. Films release, 1967). Director, Richard Rush; Screenplay, R. Wright Campbell; Cinematographer, Lazlo Kovacs; *Cast includes:* Jack Nicholson, Adam Rourke, Sabrina Scharf, Jana Taylor, John Garwood, Richard Anders, Mimi Machu. Jack plays Poet, a young gas station attendant who quits his job for the open road with a Hell's Angels motorcycle gang.

15. *Rebel Rousers* (Four Star-Excelsior release, 1967). Director, Martin B. Cohen; Screenplay, Abe Polsky, Michael Kars, and Martin B. Cohen; Cinematographer, Leslie Kouvacs (Lazlo Kovacs); *Cast includes:* Cameron Mitchell, Bruce Dern, Jack Nicholson, Diane Ladd, (Harry) Dean Stanton. Jack plays a villain in this motorcycle film, which was made while he was going through his divorce from Sandra. Bruce Dern got him the role; it's the first of four straight films they worked on together.

16. *The St. Valentine's Day Massacre* (Twentieth Century-Fox release, 1967). Director, Roger Corman; Screenplay, Howard Browne; Cinematographer, Milton Krasner; *Cast includes:* Jason Robards, George Segal, Ralph Meeker, Jean Hale, Bruce Dern,

Jack Nicholson. Jack's last film for Roger Corman. He plays a get-away driver named Gino.

17. *Psych-Out* (American International Pictures release, 1968). Director, Richard Rush; Screenplay, E. Hunter Willett and Betty Ulius; Cinematographer, Lazlo Kovacs; *Cast includes:* Susan Strasberg, Dean Stockwell, Jack Nicholson, Bruce Dern, Adam Rourke, Max Julien, Henry Jaglom, I. J. Jefferson (Mimi Machu). Jack plays a rock musician named Stony. Three scenes used in this film were written by Jack, who by this time had decided to give up acting for writing and, he hoped, directing.

18. *Head* (Columbia Pictures release, 1968). Director, Bob Rafelson; Screenplay, Bob Rafelson and Jack Nicholson; Cinematographer, Michael Hugo; *Cast includes:* Davy Jones, Mike Nesmith, Peter Tork, Micky Dolenz (the Monkees), Victor Mature, Annette Funicello, Frank Zappa, I. J. Jefferson (Mimi Machu), Bob Rafelson and Jack Nicholson (as themselves). A strange and interesting film exposing the Monkees rock group as an inane and superficial media gimmick. Jack cowrote and coproduced the film, and appeared in it briefly as himself.

19. *Easy Rider* (Columbia Pictures release, 1969). Director, Dennis Hopper; Screenplay, Peter Fonda, Dennis Hopper, and Terry Southern; Cinematographer, Lazlo Kovacs; *Cast includes:* Peter Fonda, Dennis Hopper, Jack Nicholson, Antonio Mendoza, Phil Spector, Karen Black, Robert Walker, Jr., Mac Mashourian, Sabrina Scharf, Luana Anders, Luke Askew, Warren Finnerty. The film that made Jack a star and that ended his plan to give up acting to become a director. He plays George Hanson, a disillusioned and alcoholic attorney who helps and then joins two bikers on the road in their search for America.

20. *On a Clear Day You Can See Forever* (Paramount Pictures release, 1970). Director, Vincente Minnelli; Screenplay, Alan Jay Lerner, from his play; Cinematographer, Harry Stradling; *Cast includes:* Barbra Streisand, Yves Montand, Bob Newhart, Larry Blyden, Leon Ames, Jack Nicholson, Peter Crowcroft. Jack plays Tad Pringle, Streisand's hippie stepbrother, a bit part that he took in order to work in a Vincente Minnelli musical and to capitalize on his unexpected fame.

21. *Five Easy Pieces* (Columbia Pictures release, 1970). Director,

Bob Rafelson; Screenplay, Adrien Joyce (Carol Eastman); Cinematographer, Laszlo Kovacs; *Cast includes:* Jack Nicholson, Karen Black, Susan Anspach, Lois Smith, Billy "Green" Bush, Ralph Waite, Fannie Flagg, Sally Struthers, Helena Kallianiotes, Toni Basil, Marlena MacGuire, John Ryan, William Challee. Jack plays Bobby Dupea, a former concert pianist turned drifter to get away from things that get bad if he stays in one place. A highly acclaimed film, and Jack's first feature as a star. He was nominated for an Academy Award as Best Actor for his portrayal but didn't win. It was during the making of this film that Jack had an affair with Susan Anspach, which resulted in the birth of a baby boy named Caleb, whom Jack apparently knew nothing about and whom Anspach later revealed to be Jack's son. Jack's friend Helena Kallianiotes, who sometimes doubles as his cook, household manager, and business partner, does a very humorous turn as one of two women hitchhiking to Alaska to escape filth.

22. *Carnal Knowledge* (Avco Embassy release, 1971). Director, Mike Nichols; Screenplay, Jules Feiffer; Cinematographer, Giuseppe Rotunno; *Cast includes:* Jack Nicholson, Ann-Margret, Art Garfunkel, Candice Bergen, Rita Moreno, Carol Kane. Traces the lives of two men from college to middle age, with emphasis on their inability to have mature relationships with women. This film was banned in the state of Georgia as obscene; the court later ruled that it was not. Jack lamented for years afterward that women mistook him for the character he played. He intimated that it adversely affected his casual relationships with them.

23. *A Safe Place* (Columbia Pictures release, 1971). Director, Henry Jaglom; Screenplay, Henry Jaglom; Cinematographer, Dick Kratina; *Cast includes:* Tuesday Weld, Jack Nicholson, Orson Welles, Philip Proctor. The story of a girl who is isolated by her inability to let go of the romanticized life she had been taught to expect and to accept the realities of the present. Jaglom says that Jack's highly improvisational performance is as near to the real Jack Nicholson as has ever been seen on the screen.

24. *The King of Marvin Gardens* (Columbia Pictures release, 1972). Director, Bob Rafelson; Screenplay, Jacob Brackman; Cine-

matographer, Laszlo Kovacs; *Cast includes:* Jack Nicholson, Bruce Dern, Ellen Burstyn, Benjamin "Scatman" Crothers. Jack played David Staebler, an introverted radio monologuist who gets involved with one of his brother's grandiose schemes in Atlantic City. A highly underrated film, with an excellent cast; it's considered by some to be one of Jack's best and most daring performances.

25. *The Last Detail* (Columbia Pictures release, 1973). Director, Hal Ashby; Screenplay, Robert Towne, from the Darryl Ponicsan novel; Cinematography, Michael Chapman; *Cast includes:* Jack Nicholson, Otis Young, Randy Quaid, Carol Kane. The story of two shore patrol officers who show their naïve young prisoner a good time while escorting him to prison. Jack was nominated for an Oscar for his portrayal of Billy Buddusky; it's one of Jack's favorite roles and one of his best films.

26. *Chinatown* (Paramount Pictures release, 1974). Director, Roman Polanski; Screenplay, Robert Towne; Cinematography, John A. Alonzo; *Cast includes:* Jack Nicholson, Faye Dunaway, John Huston, Perry Lopez, Diane Ladd, John Hillerman, Darrell Zwerling, Roman Polanski. Jack plays Harry Gittes, a private detective in 1930s Los Angeles in this, the first of a proposed film trilogy (part two is *The Two Jakes*) by writer Robert Towne. Towne got an Oscar for the writing. Jack was nominated for Best Actor. This film is credited by some as the one film that elevated Jack from an esteemed critical star to a major box-office one.   191

27. *The Passenger* [*Professione: Reporter*] (Metro-Goldwyn-Mayer release, 1975). Director, Michelangelo Antonioni; Screenplay, Mark Peploe, Peter Wollen, and Michelangelo Antonioni; Cinematographer, Luciano Tovoli; *Cast includes:* Jack Nicholson, Maria Schneider, Jenny Runacre, Ian Hendry, Steven Berkoff, James Campbell, Ambrose Bia, Chuck Mulvehill. Jack plays David Locke, a political reporter so frustrated with the treadmill of his own existence that he assumes the identity of a recently-deceased man who bears a resemblance to him. A good film, renowned among buffs for its uncut seven-minute tracking shot at the end. Jack was given the *Harvard Lampoon* Golden Thumbscrew Award for once again playing an "identity crisis."

28. *Tommy* (Columbia Pictures release, 1975). Director, Ken Russell; Screenplay, Ken Russell, from the rock opera by The Who; Cinematography, Dick Bush and Ronnie Taylor, *Cast includes:* Ann-Margret, Roger Daltry, Oliver Reed, Elton John, Keith Moon, Jack Nicholson. Jack did a cameo and a little singing as a medical doctor.

29. *The Fortune* (Columbia Pictures release, 1975). Director, Mike Nichols; Screenplay, Adrien Joyce (Carol Eastman); Cinematographer, John A. Alonzo; *Cast includes:* Jack Nicholson, Warren Beatty, Stockard Channing, Florence Stanley. Jack plays a dim-witted con man in this underrated comedy. It was during the filming of this picture that he learned the truth about his birth.

30. *One Flew Over the Cuckoo's Nest* (United Artists release, 1975). Director, Milos Forman; Screenplay, Laurence Hauben and Bo Goldman, from Ken Kesey's novel; Cinematographers, Haskell Wexler and Bill Butler; *Cast includes:* Jack Nicholson, Louise Fletcher, William Redfield, Will Sampson, Benjamin "Scatman" Crothers, Brad Dourif, Danny DeVito. Jack won an Oscar for his performance as Randle Patrick McMurphy, a prison inmate who cons his way into a psychiatric hospital for a "vacation" and becomes the inmates' champion. The film was awarded an Oscar as Best Picture, as were Louise Fletcher (Best Actress) and Milos Forman (Best Director).

31. *The Missouri Breaks* (United Artists release, 1976). Director, Arthur Penn; Screenplay, Thomas McGuane; Cinematographer, Michael Butler; *Cast includes:* Marlon Brando, Jack Nicholson, Randy Quaid, Kathleen Lloyd, Harry Dean Stanton. Jack plays a cattle rustler to Brando's hired gun in this offbeat Western, which most critics disliked.

32. *The Last Tycoon* (Paramount Pictures release, 1976). Director, Elia Kazan; Screenplay, Harold Pinter, from F. Scott Fitzgerald's novel; Cinematographer, Victor Kemper; *Cast includes:* Robert De Niro, Ingrid Boulting, Robert Mitchum, Jeanne Moreau, Jack Nicholson. Jack plays a small role as a Communist union organizer named Brimmer.

33. *Goin' South* (Paramount Pictures release, 1978). Director, Jack Nicholson; Screenplay, John Herman Shaner, Al Ramus,

Charles Shyer, and Alan Mandel; Cinematographer, Néstor Almendros; *Cast includes:* Jack Nicholson, Mary Steenburgen, Christopher Lloyd, John Belushi, Veronica Cartwright, Jeff Morris. Jack's second effort as a director. A romantic comedy set in the post–Civil War West. Jack plays Henry Moon, a bank robber and horse thief saved from the gallows by marriage. Jack's uncle, George "Shorty" Smith, has a bit part as a neighbor who with his wife and another couple visit the Moons.

34. *The Shining* (Warner Brothers release, 1980).) Director, Stanley Kubrick; Screenplay, Stanley Kubrick and Diane Johnson, from the novel by Stephen King; Cinematographer, John Alcott; *Cast includes:* Jack Nicholson, Shelley Duvall, Danny Lloyd, Benjamin "Scatman" Crothers. Jack plays Jack Torrance, a would-be novelist who, with his wife and son, takes a job as caretaker of a closed mountain hotel and is driven mad by the spirits who haunt the place. Jack wrote the scene in which Torrance is enraged when his wife interrupts his writing—a recreation of an incident in his own marriage with Sandra Knight. He also added the film's most memorable line: "Here's Johnny!"

35. *The Postman Always Rings Twice* (Paramount Pictures release, 1981). Director, Bob Rafelson; Screenplay, David Mamet, from the James M. Cain novel; Cinematographer, Sven Nykvist; *Cast includes:* Jack Nicholson, Jessica Lange, John Colicos, Michael Lerner, Anjelica Huston. A remake of the Tay Garnett–directed 1946 film. Jack plays Frank Chambers, a masochistic drifter whose lust for another man's wife leads him to join the wife in a plot to kill the husband.

36. *Reds* (Paramount Pictures release, 1981). Director, Warren Beatty; Screenplay, Warren Beatty and Trevor Griffiths; Cinematographer, Vittorio Storaro; *Cast includes:* Warren Beatty, Diane Keaton, Maureen Stapleton, Jack Nicholson, Paul Sorvino, Gene Hackman. Jack plays a cameo as American playwright Eugene O'Neill in this true love story of American journalists John Reed and Louise Bryant, set against the Russian Revolution.

37. *The Border* (Universal release, 1981). Director, Tony Richardson; Screenplay, Deric Washburn, Walon Green, and David Freeman; Cinematographer, Ric Waite; *Cast includes:* Jack

193

Nicholson, Valerie Perrine, Harvey Keitel, Warren Oates. Jack plays Charlie Smith, a border-patrol officer on the Mexican-American border, in this action melodrama.

38. *Terms of Endearment* (Paramount Pictures release, 1983). Director, James L. Brooks; Screenplay, James L. Brooks, from the Larry McMurtry novel; Cinematographer, Andrzej Bartkowiak; *Cast includes:* Shirley MacLaine, Debra Winger, Jack Nicholson, Jeff Daniels, John Lithgow, Danny DeVito. Jack won an Oscar as Best Supporting Actor for his role as former astronaut Garrett Breedlove in this comedy-drama about a mother-daughter relationship. The film was named Best Picture by the Academy. Shirley MacLaine won an Oscar as Best Actress, and Brooks won two—for directing and for his screen adaptation.

39. *Prizzi's Honor* (Twentieth Century-Fox release, 1985). Director, John Huston; Screenplay, Richard Condon and Janet Roach, from the Richard Condon novel; Cinematographer, Andrzej Bartkowiak; *Cast includes:* Jack Nicholson, Kathleen Turner, Anjelica Huston, William Hickey. Jack plays Charley Partanna, a slow-witted Mafia hit man in this dark comedy. Anjelica won an Oscar as Best Supporting Actress for her role as Maerose, and John Huston became the first director ever to guide both a parent (his father, Walter—in *The Treasure of the Sierra Madre*) and an offspring (Anjelica) in Oscar-winning performances.

40. *Heartburn* (Paramount Pictures release, 1986). Director, Mike Nichols; Screenplay, Nora Ephron, from her novel; Cinematographer, Néstor Almendros; *Cast includes:* Meryl Streep, Jack Nicholson, Jeff Daniels, Maureen Stapleton, Stockard Channing, Richard Masur, Catherine O'Hara. Jack plays a philandering husband in what is alleged to be a thinly disguised account of Nora Ephron's marriage breakup with journalist Carl Bernstein.

41. *The Witches of Eastwick* (Warner Brothers release, 1987). Director, George Miller; Screenplay, Michael Cristofer, based very loosely on John Updike's novel; Cinematographer, Vilmos Zsigmond; *Cast includes:* Jack Nicholson, Cher, Susan Sarandon, Michelle Pfeiffer. Jack plays the Devil incarnate, Darryl Van Horne, in this humorous battle-of-the-sexes fantasy.

42. *Ironweed* (Tri-Star Pictures release, 1987). Director, Hector

194

Babenco; Screenplay, William Kennedy, from his novel; Cinematographer, Lauro Escorel; Cast includes: Jack Nicholson, Meryl Streep, Carroll Baker, Tom Waits, Michael O'Keeffe. A grim but fascinating view of 1930s street people that was deserving of far more attention than it got. Jack plays an alcoholic drifter, Francis Phelan, who returns to Albany, New York, and again faces the past from which he had fled. Both Jack and Meryl Streep were deservedly nominated for Oscars, but failed to win. There are particularly fine performances also by Tom Waits and Carroll Baker.

43. Broadcast News (Twentieth Century-Fox release, 1987). Director, James L. Brooks; Screenplay, James L. Brooks; Cinematographer, Michael Ballhaus; Cast includes: William Hurt, Albert Brooks, Holly Hunter, Jack Nicholson, Robert Prosky, Lois Chiles, Joan Cusack. Jack does a walk-on as a superstar network news anchorman in this hugely successful film about the television news business.

44. Batman (Warner Brothers release, 1989). Director, Tim Burton; Screenplay, Warren Skaaren and Sam Hamm; Cinematographer, Roger Pratt; Cast includes: Michael Keaton, Jack Nicholson, Kim Basinger, Robert Wuhl, Michael Gough. Jack plays Jack Napier, a small-time gangster who emerges as the Joker after Batman throws him into a vat of toxic waste in this adventure of cartoonist Bob Kane's comic-book hero.

45. The Two Jakes (Paramount Pictures release, 1990). Director, Jack Nicholson; Screenplay, Robert Towne; Cinematographer, Vilmos Zsigmond; Cast includes: Jack Nicholson, Harvey Keitel, Meg Tilly, Madeleine Stowe, Rubén Blades, Frederic Forrest, Eli Wallach, Rebecca Broussard. Jack again plays Los Angeles private detective Jake Gittes in this sequel to Chinatown, which is the second film of a planned trilogy of original screenplays by Robert Towne. Rebecca Broussard, who gave birth to Jack's child before the film's release, plays his secretary. This is Jack's third directorial effort.

The following films were directed by Jack Nicholson:

1. Drive, He Said (Columbia Pictures release, 1970). Director, Jack Nicholson; Screenplay, Jack Nicholson and Jeremy Larner, from Larner's novel; Cinematographer, Bill Butler; Cast in-

cludes: William Tepper, Karen Black, Michael Margotta, Bruce Dern, Robert Towne, Henry Jaglom.
2. *Goin' South* (see listing number 33, films of).
3. *The Two Jakes* (see listing number 45, films of).

The following films were written by Jack Nicholson:
1. *Thunder Island* (Twentieth Century-Fox release, 1963). Director, Jack Leewood; Screenplay, Jack Nicholson and Don Devlin; Cinematographer, John Nickolaus; *Cast includes:* Gene Nelson, Fay Spain, Brian Kelly. The story of an American underworld figure who is hired to assassinate a deposed Latin American dictator. One reviewer called the script better than average for a B picture.
2. *Flight to Fury* (see listing number 11, films of).
3. *Ride in the Whirlwind* (see listing number 13, films of).
4. *The Trip* (American International Pictures release, 1967). Director, Roger Corman; Screenplay, Jack Nicholson; Cinematographer, Archie Dalzell; *Cast includes:* Peter Fonda, Susan Strasberg, Bruce Dern, Dennis Hopper. Jack drew from elements of his own life and his experiences with LSD to write this screenplay about a young TV-commercial director facing separation from his wife. Jack wrote the part of John, the drug guru, for himself, but Bruce Dern was given the role. This and other experiences convinced him that his place was behind the camera, as director, and it was at about this time that he decided to give up acting.
5. *Head* (see listing number 18, films of).
6. *Drive, He Said* (see listing number 1, directed by).

The following films were coproduced by Jack Nicholson:
1. *The Shooting,* coproduced with Monte Hellman (see listing number 12, films of).
2. *Ride in the Whirlwind,* coproduced with Monte Hellman (see listing number 13, films of).
3. *Head,* coproduced with Bob Rafelson (see listing number 18, films of).

INDEX

199

203